WOOD-CARVING
AS A HOBBY

Carved oak chest, executed by Mr. James W. Williams, instructor in history, after two lessons in wood-carving.

WOOD-CARVING AS A HOBBY

BY

HERBERT W. FAULKNER, Ph.B.,M.E.

Steel to Steel sharpens
OLD ADAGE

Foreword
by
Earnest Elmo Calkins

HARPER & BROTHERS PUBLISHERS
NEW YORK AND LONDON

WOOD-CARVING AS A HOBBY

Fourth Edition

I-K

To

QUEENE FERRY COONLEY

this volume

is affectionately dedicated by

The Author

CONTENTS

FOREWORD by Earnest Elmo Calkins   ix

PREFACE   xiii

I. INTRODUCTION   1

II. TOOLS   12

III. CARVING IN LOW RELIEF   23

IV. CARVING IN HIGH RELIEF   32

V. WOODS SUITABLE TO CARVE   41

VI. DESIGNS FOR WOOD-CARVING   50

VII. TECHNIQUE AND FINISH   60

VIII. CARVING IN THE ROUND   70

IX. CARVING IN THE GOTHIC MANNER   79

X. RENAISSANCE CARVING   90

XI. CARVED MOULDINGS   110

XII. CARVED LETTERING   121

XIII. VARIOUS SUGGESTIONS   127

INDEX   139

FOREWORD

BY

EARNEST ELMO CALKINS

I KNOW of no man better fitted to write a book about wood-carving than Herbert Faulkner. He is beautifully equipped with the three essentials, the conscience of the craftsman, the taste of the artist, and the ability to express his ideas in clear and simple language so desirable in a book that is to be at once a guide and an inspiration.

He makes his instruction practicable and understandable without neglecting the philosophy which should lie behind every craft practiced more for its therapeutic effect upon the practicer than for any value of the products. For wood-carving is a cure for many of our social ills. As the old Grand Rapids wood-carver observed: "You have to have a good disposition to work in wood." The point is, that you have it, or you get it; for there is a tonic quality in the feel of chisel against block, in that contest between your mastery of the tool and the wilfulness of the grain, that renders you for the time being wholly oblivious to all earthly cares.

As a spare-time occupation it has many virtues, not the least being the ease with which it can be sandwiched between duties or tasks as a refresher, when another set of faculties has become jaded with use. The project is clamped to the bench—and any good-sized box makes a bench—awaiting your leisure, ready at all times; you step in, pick up your chisel, go on from where you left off. It particularly fits the sedentary life, yielding a mild exercise—I have worked up a perspiration removing the superfluous material from a large block—and affording that teamwork between hand, eye and brain which is the most satisfying combination, the most rewarding exercise.

One of its charms—and this applies to all crafts followed as hobbies—is that there is no discouraging standard of perfection with which you must compete. You do what you do for your own approval, and for that of no one else. You will enjoy your little triumphs and victories, and they will yield a satisfaction out of all proportion to the results achieved. The reward comes, not from beating a professional wood-carver, but in bettering your own skill; though it should never be forgotten that in this and all arts there is no limit, no rule holding you back. You are at liberty to make yourself as expert as you can, to go as far as you like, perhaps discover in yourself a hidden and unsuspected bent for this form of self-expression if such there be. That would be agreeable, but it is not necessary for complete enjoyment of the craft. Wood-carving has delights and surprises all along the road from novice to expert. It is one of the most rewarding of the crafts —clean, honest, sturdy, of distinguished lineage, and appealing to the finest instincts.

You will find Mr. Faulkner a competent and dependable teacher. He is an artist of note and distinction. Wood-carving is one of his many accomplishments. He has taught it for years and understands the beginner's viewpoint. He has taste and artistic integrity, and a genuine enthusiasm for this fine old handcraft, which should not be permitted to perish from the earth under the blight of the machine. He will lead you into pleasant hours and fresh interests and restore your soul; for intimate first-hand knowledge of a craft opens new doors on life, and links you with one of the noblest aspects of human endeavor, the long line of skills and crafts by which the hand of man has added beauty to the world.

PREFACE

THIS book is written for the man, woman, boy or girl, who has a taste for the use of tools and leisure to enjoy the same; to show these craftsmen that wood-carving is a creative art simple to learn, and delightful to practice; to provide the designs, the woods and the necessary tools, and to state the few and simple rules to be followed.

In preparing this book, the writer has received encouragement from Earnest Elmo Calkins, Esq., the inspiration to write, and the opportunity to publish this volume. Thanks are here cordially offered him for this, as well as for his kindness in consenting to write the introduction.

Thanks are offered also to Roderic Barbour Barnes, Esq., architect, for his encouragement in giving the author an opportunity to execute decorative wood-carving on a large scale for the embellishment of a beautiful home.

James Gamble Rogers, Esq., architect, has also kindly helped by furnishing information concerning the carvings at Yale University, for which I express my appreciation.

And encouragement has come from the many pupils: artists, schoolboys and girls, teachers, carpenters and chauffeurs, soldiers and nurses, all of whom have ardently and ably responded to the instruction received. They have stimulated me to write for the benefit of a larger circle of craftsmen beyond the reach of personal instruction.

HERBERT W. FAULKNER

WOOD-CARVING
AS A HOBBY

CHAPTER I

INTRODUCTION

ALL of us have our vocations and our avocations, the one which we follow through necessity, the other we pursue with enthusiasm. Avocations are frequently referred to as "hobbies," or fast horses, but make-believe ones, which the rider mounts and gallops without arriving anywhere. But if the imaginary horse can give the illusion of real speed, the exhilaration and quickening pulse, it serves the rider well, and justifies its existence.

People who are clever with their hands can find many a welcome hobbyhorse to carry them through their leisure hours, and one of the most simple of these is Wood-Carving. I venture to call it a simple craft because the equipment is small and the rules are few. One needs only leisure, interest in the subject, a few tools, patience and willingness to observe the three simple rules. Any person who can sharpen a pencil can learn to carve wood, but he who has experience in the use of carpenter's tools has a better preparation.

Dexterity with tools is of great value, but more important still is the discovery that it is possible to shape a rough piece of wood into any form desired. This is precisely what the wood-carver undertakes to do, and the realization that this is perfectly easy of accomplishment makes all the future labor light. But while the carpenter must adhere strictly to the drawings given him, the wood-carver, enjoying greater freedom, interprets his design as his taste and experience dictate. If the student can get to realize that he has it in his power to carve any design he pleases, the chief difficulty is already overcome. The rest of his training is but the learning of a few technicalities, applied with patience and perseverance.

The purpose of carving wood is to make the surface more interesting through imposing a graceful pattern upon it, and inducing an interesting play of light and shadow, pleasant to contemplate.

At one time, during the nineteenth century, our furniture and woodwork became intricate and overloaded with ornament, most of which was machine-made and appliqué, that is, fastened on with glue, and often destined to fall off.

A reaction against this redundancy produced the so-called "Mission Style" of heavy, but well-constructed furniture entirely denuded of ornament.

Then came a revival of Colonial and Early American furniture, the examples in oak being ornamented with carving, those in mahogany generally plain befitting that wood, rich in color and taking a lovely polished surface. The excellence of this early American craftsmanship has revived an interest in good hand-carving. From museums we may copy those excellent designs, while in many homes we may enjoy the pleasing effect of the carving and appraise its value for decoration.

As I look up from writing, my eyes rest upon a band of moulding over the fireplace which was designed and carved in France perhaps two hundred years ago by some clever craftsman long forgotten, whose work lives to tell of his enjoyment in his labors. A vine emerges from the solid, lifeless wood, to curve and twist in graceful undulations, its leaves as suave and crisp as those outside my window, and here and there flowers bloom, pushing out from the shadows as the arbutus flowers peep from the moss in spring. When evening comes to veil the design, I am still conscious of a rich play of light and shade that makes the fireplace more welcome to contemplate. The band of carving is not in any way pictorial, but admirably decorative, and we see that the craftsman was an artist who knew how to follow nature without slavishly copying it.

In carving wood, the purpose is not to produce wooden pictures, as the Swiss attempt to do, and fail, in spite of their amazing cleverness and dexterity. The ultimate end is to produce a decorative pattern on the wood which will make the surface interesting; but the immediate purpose is to *carve*; to compel some gracious form to reveal itself, as if it were hidden there by some spell in the solid wood, waiting to be evoked by the magic of our carving tools. We who learn how to release the hidden forms become heirs and kin to the great sculptors and artists, and share with them the rapture of creating something new and beautiful.

We know our work will be a joy for years to come, as is my fireplace decoration, an inheritance out of the past. Perhaps the trees, whose wood we are to carve, have been growing for a century or more, building up massive trunks in which lie imprisoned, like dryads, the forms and designs we liberate. And it is our business and pleasure to learn the methods and acquire the skill to accomplish the surprising feat of liberation, to break the spell which binds them, and set them free.

But certain obstacles confront us which we must recognize and vanquish, chief of which come from the resistance and the peculiarities of the wood. Woods of all kinds have a fiber traversing their substance, and a grain made up of layers of annual growth. Cuts made at random in the wood are apt to split and splinter it. In order to make a clean and precise shape, the carver must take out clean chips, and to do this he must first sever the grain.

If you watch a woodchopper fell a tree, you will observe that he scatters clean-cut chips, each one made by two strokes of his axe, the first horizontal, the second slanting downward. Watch also an expert whittler and notice that he, too, expends two cuts to make every chip. The woodchopper and the whittler are applying the first rule of wood-carving, which is:

Rule I: First sever the grain of the wood, then cut out a clean chip. The first stroke we call the "stop-cut," A, in Fig. 1, the second "the slice," B.

Where some wood has been removed, the opening

may serve as a stop-cut, and may be enlarged and shaped by slicing into it from all sides, as in C.

Rule II: Consider the grain of the wood and make the slice in a direction to bring the tool out clean, not into the wood which splits it. As you cut, the chip should curl away from the tool, as in C. The sharpening of a pencil in D, is an excellent application of Rule II. We know that we must not sharpen a pencil from the point *upward*, but must slice *downward* at an oblique

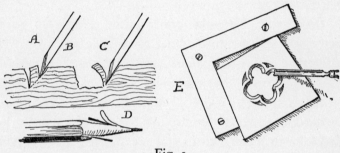

Fig. 1

angle, making the chips curl downward from the knife. Cutting in the opposite direction would split the wood and ruin our pencil. In planing a board, we see to it that we plane away from the grain, or we shall dig up the wood and roughen the surface instead of smoothing it. It may help to an understanding of this important matter of direction if we imagine that the grain of the wood is like frozen ruts in a road, and that a chauffeur in traveling over it, is constantly trying to turn the wheels of his car out of the ruts, not into them. The tool, like the car, should turn constantly out of the grooves toward the open spaces.

Rule III: Never place the left hand in front of the tool, for tools are sharp, and they may slip or split through the wood and cruelly gash the hand standing in the way. A moment of forgetfulness may cause anguish at the time, and discouragement for the future.

Position: When working with the mallet, we grasp and guide the blade with the left hand while striking with the right—Fig. 2. But at other times we hold the

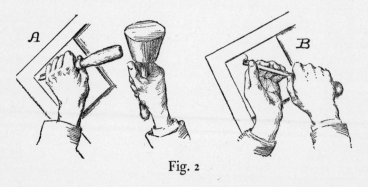

Fig. 2

handle in the right hand and push the tool toward the left while the left hand, holding the tool near the tip, guides its direction and regulates the forward motion, as in B. In either case the left hand stands back of the keen cutting edge, and is safe from possible harm. For the sake of the hand and the work, neither tool nor wood must be permitted to slip. We may hold the work in a vise, or clamp it to the work-bench, but either plan involves loosening it every time we need to change its position to make our slices in obedience to Rule II.

I like to have my work at once free to move and

firm from slipping, and this I accomplish by means of a stop or cleat on the work-bench to push the wood against when making a slice. Better still are two cleats, at right angles to each another, screwed to the work-bench, as shown in the Fig. 1, E. Where there is no danger of slipping, there is no excuse for disregarding Rule III. Pupils who cut their hands more than once should be forbidden to continue carving!

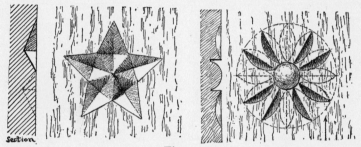

Section

Fig. 3

First Exercise: Let us carve an incised star, Fig. 3, in order to learn the proper direction of the slices in reference to the direction of the grain of the wood. On a smooth block describe a circle about 2 inches in diameter, divide the circumference into five equal parts and construct within it a regular, inscribed star of five points. Through the center draw radial lines from each point to the reentrant angle opposite, thus dividing the star into five irregular diamonds, or lozenge-shaped sections, and join all the reentrant angles with lines forming a small pentagon. Our star is now split up into 20 small triangles, each one of which is to be dug out with a chisel. But stop-cuts must first be made the length of each diamond and across it, placing the point of a sharp knife where lines intersect in the middle, pressing deep down and slanting upward to each apex of the diamond. Now clean, triangular chips may be taken, slicing from the hypotenuse of each triangle downward and inward with a slanting cut, till you meet the stop-cut well below the surface. A few trials will show you the direction to take with the chisel, for cutting with the grain will bring out a neat little triangle and leave a smooth incline. But if the wrong direction is chosen a split will occur which may break through into an adjoining compartment. Attention must be concentrated on this matter of the direction of the grain of the wood.

Next we should carve a design made up of curved slices. The pattern of a daisy, or "Black-eyed Susan," is recommended for this exercise, shown in Fig. 3. Describe on the wood a 2-inch circle and divide it into 12 equal parts with that number of radii. Draw a circle of ½ inch diameter for the eye, and form the rays with arcs of ½ inch radius beginning at the edge of the eye, meeting and terminating at the twelve points on the larger circle. Choose a gouge which exactly fits the curve of the inner circle, and make a deep, vertical stop-cut all around it. Then, turning the gouge face downward, slice with a curving stroke from the center downward and outward, digging a circular groove. Continue to take thin slices from the eye, forming it into a little, rounded dome appearing like a bullet sunken deep in the surrounding wood. You will have frequent occasion to carve little domes like this, as they are an often-repeated motive in designs for wood-carving and are known as "pearls."

The rays are to be hollowed out like the hulls of little boats. Each calls for a stop-cut from point to point, down the center line ¼ inch to the keel. With a gouge slice out half a ray, making sure that you cut away from the grain. Now turn the block about and slice the other half of the ray in the opposite direction. Repeat the above process in all the eight rays which lie diagonally with reference to the grain of the wood.

In Fig. 3 these eight rays are shown with half their wood already sliced out, before turning the block. The up-and-down rays must be cut downward from each pointed end. The rays lying across the grain must be sliced from the widest part of the curved outline downward and inward to the keel.

This exercise will impress upon the student the proper direction to make the slice, and accustom him to take the right direction, instantly and without conscious effort.

Incised designs like the foregoing are not so common as these where the pattern appears as an ornament in relief against a sunken background. Our exercise will, therefore, be the carving of a rosette in relief —Fig. 4. The design, about 2½ inches square, is sketched out on the wood and about ⅟₁₆ inch outside the perimeter a vertical stop-cut ¼ inch deep is made with chisel and mallet, then with the same tools we cut a furrow all around. With a gouge, all the wood is cut away around the square, and to a depth of ¼ inch, and the rough surface so formed must be smoothed down with a carpenter's chisel. This tool will act precisely like a smoothing plane if the bevel is rubbed forward and backward over the block; for the cutting edge will slice off projections, while the bevel prevents it from digging in. With patience and care an even,

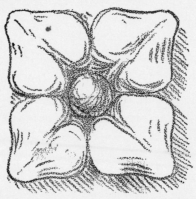

Fig. 4

flat background can be made, leaving the square projecting boldly from it.

The central pearl should now be carved, as explained in the last exercise. And this must be separated from the bases of the surrounding leaves by carving an inclined channel all around it. Next, the narrow wood must be sliced away from the graceful outline, using a gouge, and cutting at a slight incline outward, so that the base is a little larger than the surface. Lastly, the four leaves should be slightly rounded downward, and a groove cut in the middle of each to represent a midrib, deepest at the pearl and growing shallower at the tip.

If the student executes these exercises, neatly and without accident, finding, at the same time, enjoyment in the labor, he may venture to extend his equipment and attempt more ambitious projects.

CHAPTER II

TOOLS

THUS far I have mentioned no special tools, knowing that the simple exercises given can be carried out with ordinary gouges and chisels. The beautiful carvings

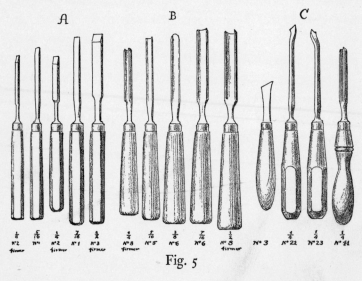

Fig. 5

made during the Middle Ages were undoubtedly executed with crude tools, few in number and most likely made by village blacksmiths. Today the dealer offers us tools of the finest steel, highly finished, and in such variety as to make the choice embarrassing. The collections on sale, with uniform handles of polished

12

wood, reposing in neat tool boxes, are alluring to the
beginner, but experience shows that such collections
are likely to contain some unnecessary tools, and to
lack other desirable ones. The uniformity of the handles is also an objection, as will be explained.

A "kit" of fourteen tools has served me for all my
work, with the addition of one extra-large gouge for
the boldest carving, and a tiny gouge and chisel for
the very finest, making seventeen at the most. The
collection recommended is made up of five gouges,
five chisels and four special carving tools, shown in
Fig. 5. The chisels are of two kinds: The ordinary carpenter's chisel, somewhat thick and beveled by grinding on one side only, known as a "firmer chisel," and
the carving chisel, thinner, shorter and usually slightly
narrower at the handle than at the tip. This latter is
ground on both upper and lower faces.

LIST OF TOOLS

Carving Chisels:		Firmer Chisels:	
5/16 wide	No. 1	1/8 wide	No. 2
7/16 "	No. 1	1/4 "	No. 2
		1/2 "	No. 3

The gouges offered in the shops are made in 12 widths
from 1/16 inch to one inch, and each width may have
one of nine curvatures or "sweeps," making 108 patterns to choose from, the sweep being indicated by a
number. We need gouges of greater and smaller sweeps
for cutting the varying curvatures in outline and
surface of our design.

Carving Gouges:		Firmer Gouges:	
5/16 wide	No. 5	1/4 wide	No. 8
3/8 "	No. 6	1/2 "	No. 8
7/16 "	No. 6		

The dealer will furnish a chart showing the sweeps of all the gouges to be had, from which the student may choose the blades he is most likely to require. Numbers indicate curvature, measurements indicate width.

The four special tools are: The veining tool, which makes a V-shaped cut.

1/4 inch wide veining tool	No. 41
1/4 inch spoon chisel right bend	No. 22
1/4 " " " left "	No. 23
1/2 " wood-carving knife	No. 3

Besides the 108 gouges above mentioned, there are numberless tools on the dealers' lists which look attractively professional but may be dispensed with entirely. In the catalogue are pictured sweep-chisels and sweep-gouges; there are tools long-bent, back-bent and spoon-shaped; also, there are spoon-parting tools, in all numbering about 336.

A friend gave me some of these odd-shaped tools more than twenty years ago, and I confess I have never found need for them in my work.

Chisels. Since chisels have straight cutting edges, they are suited for cutting straight lines and carving flat planes, and for blocking out convex round projections, but are not adapted for scooping out hollow curved forms.

Gouges. Gouges are the proper tools for carving these forms, as well as for finishing convex curved lines and surfaces. That gouge should be used whose sweep most nearly corresponds to the curvature of the line or surface to be cut.

Special Tools. Bent chisels are designed to slice out chips from difficult corners, and are therefore made "rights and lefts" so as to serve in either direction. Like pistols, they are not often needed, but occasionally greatly so.

The veining tool is necessary for making shallow grooves and for finishing deeper ones. Used upon a wood like chestnut, where hard and soft grains occur side by side, the veining tool may swerve from the drawn line and waver as it encounters a varying resistance. This annoyance may be alleviated by first making a stop-cut all along the middle of the groove that is to be. The veining tool will more readily keep to the proper line with this preliminary cut to guide it. Shallow grooves may generally be cut in any direction without reference to the grain of the wood, provided the tool is thoroughly sharp, but when we cut deep grooves obliquely to the grain, we discover that our veining tool is cutting away from the grain on one side, but digging into it on the other, making a rough cut of the latter. To avoid this difficulty, make a deep stop-cut down the middle of the groove, incline the veining tool over to the side where the grain permits a clean cut, and slice that side only. Then, by turning the work about end for end, the other side of the groove may be sliced out, since, in the new position, the wood presents a favorable approach to the tool (see Fig. 6). This plan of cutting a groove, first on one side then on the other, is particularly useful in carving curved furrows.

Circles are particularly troublesome to carve sharply and neatly, and the preliminary stop-cut all around will be found of great assistance. Two opposite points are particularly troublesome (see Fig. 7), where the tool for a moment follows the grain, and is disinclined to turn and follow the line desired, and like a stubborn animal, seems determined to slide off along the grain.

Fig. 6   Fig. 7

But the carver, being forewarned, can master the situation through firmly controlling his tool. The grooved circle is a valuable motive in decorative carving, when accurately and neatly executed, and the student should train his hand to do this work in a manner approaching perfection.

Knives. The wood-carving knife, shown at C, Fig. 5, is a tool of great utility, especially for making stop-cuts deeper at one end than at the other, as we saw in carving the star. It is not strictly a knife, but more properly speaking, a thin chisel, with a slanting edge and a sharply pointed tip. I am often told of pieces of carving "done entirely with a jackknife," but the few examples I have seen consist of a loose ring on a stick, a ball inside of a cage, and a clumsy chain, all articles of no practical use and no decorative value. Lacking other tools, but possessing infinite patience, the determined craftsman may force himself to carve certain motives with his jackknife, provided they are convex surfaces bounded by approximately straight outlines. Hollow curved depressions cannot, in their very nature, be scooped out with a jackknife, at least not with any accuracy or finish. Suave curves of vines and crisp edges of flowers, well-rounded fruits, rippling surfaces of leaves are beyond the scope of the jackknife, and today, when so many useful tools are available, it is absurd for a carver to use an implement so crude as the jackknife.

Handles. It is a good plan to have variety rather than uniformity among the handles of the tools. I can recognize in an instant the tool desired, because the handle identifies each one. Thus I save precious time and press along the work with speed. I have all the gouges mounted in simple, turned handles, the ends being somewhat flattened to receive mallet strokes. Chisel handles I make octagonal, and flattened in the same manner. My four special tools are mounted in handles of varied distinguishing shapes.

Scraper. Besides the foregoing, there is a tool belonging strictly to the carpenter, but which is often of great use to the wood-carver, namely, the scraper. It consists of a thin, rectangular piece of steel, about 2 inches wide and 3½ long. The two shorter edges are the cutting edges, which are first ground perpendicular to the surfaces, and then rubbed and polished on the oilstones till they shine like silver. Then a round steel rod is rubbed backward and forward against all the ground edges in such a manner as to turn over the

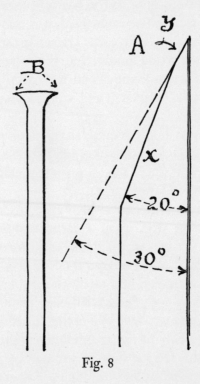

Fig. 8

steel all along, and form tiny curved scraping edges, two at each end of our scraper, as shown in Fig. 8-B. Dragged over the surface of wood, this scraping edge will take off slight roughnesses and projections, and when desired, it will also remove a design drawn on the wood, without resort to the plane.

Sandpaper. Sandpaper (so called, though actually made with crushed glass) must be strictly avoided by the wood-carver for several reasons, one of which I wish to emphasize here. When sandpaper is rubbed over the surface of wood it not only smooths it, but at the same time leaves embedded in it minute particles of glass forming a fine grit. Thereafter, tools cutting into the gritty wood quickly lose their sharpness. Keep this in mind in ordering wood for carving, and insist that the surface be planed and scraped only, but never sandpapered.

Sharpening. Tools require sharpening when newly purchased, and constant upkeep as they become dulled. Sharpening is in three stages: grinding, rubbing on oil-stones, stropping on leather.

Grinding is done on a revolving stone moistened with water, or dry, upon a carborundum wheel. In either case, the face of the wheel must turn away from the tool. The ground surface is never bright and shiny because it is scraped and channeled by the roughness of the grinder, and the beveled edge produced cannot be a keen cutting edge. We could, with time and patience, rub away all the roughnesses from the ground bevel, but this fatigue may be avoided by merely rubbing on the oilstone and producing a fine, narrow cutting edge at the extreme tip of the tool. Fig. 8-A represents the section of a tool blade which has been ground to an angle of 20°, x representing the ground bevel. Then the tip, y, has been rubbed till bright and sharp on the oilstone, making an angle of 30°. The soft, gray stone, with plenty of oil, should be used first, followed by the hard, white one, and additional keenness is given on a piece of leather dusted with finest emery powder. If the grindstone or wheel has a tool-rest, this will help greatly in maintaining the tool at the proper angle. The grinder being circular, tends to grind a hollow into the steel. To avoid this, the tool must be frequently examined, and the position changed to make a smooth surface of the proper angle. Chisels should have even, flat planes, gouges should be constantly turned from side to side so as to grind a smooth cylindrical surface, having the same curvature as the gouge, not spoon-shaped, nor having any angles nor planes. The nose of the gouge must be square across, with sharp angles, not rounding like the letter U. One gouge, however, should be an exception to the rule, and may have the U-shaped end, for it is occasionally desirable to use a round-nosed tool. The middle gouge of our set is represented in Fig. 5 as ground in this manner.

The spoon chisels are ground like other chisels, save that the bevel is ground at an angle so as to produce a sharp point at the outer end. The veining tool is the most difficult tool of all to grind, as the nose must be kept square, and the two bevels must meet below, exactly in the middle of the V-shaped groove.

The wood-carving knife presents no great difficulty. Being thin, it requires little or no grinding upon the wheel, and is easily finished on the oilstone. But we must take pains to keep the edge at an angle to the center line of the blade with a sharp point projecting forward. In course of time the bevels of tools become somewhat rounded, and must be corrected by grinding, and the new cutting edge sharpened. The water on the grindstone prevents the friction from heating the tool and spoiling its temper, but the carborundum wheel is inclined to heat up. The moment a tool feels hot to the hand, it should be instantly popped into water to cool and save the temper of the steel.

There are two grades of oilstones needed to give extreme sharpness to the tools: the one called Washita is light gray in color, and somewhat soft; the other, The Hard Arkansas, white like marble, and decidedly harder. They should have wooden covers to protect them from grit, and need to be wiped clean before the oil is applied. Two or three "clips" of the harder stone, curved and also wedge-shaped, are desirable for retouching the inside curve of gouges and groove of the veining tool, in case the edges get turned over in a burr in the sharpening. A "feather edge" sometimes comes while grinding, and this must be removed by vertical grinding and a resumption of the whole sharpening process.

If by accident a tool gets nicked, it requires a major operation. This is performed by holding the tool vertically against the wheel, and grinding it straight across till the nick disappears. Then a new bevel must be ground and a new cutting edge formed. When one is eager to carve, he must possess considerable firmness of purpose to spend precious time upon dull tools and monotonous grinding. But he will reap his reward later when he sees a rough block of wood melt away under his keen tools, and feels the chips fly or curl away from smoothly carved surfaces, and beholds graceful outlines emerging as his work proceeds.

Save the cutting edges and you save all! Take great care never to drop a tool on the floor, and when you finally cease your carving, store the tools carefully away in such a manner that no harm can come to their keen edges. Your fourteen tools may be conveniently and safely stored in a roll of some soft, thick cloth, having a series of fourteen pockets, one for each blade, and a flap to fold over the handles.

One more tool remains to be mentioned: the mallet. An old croquet mallet, with handle cut to convenient length will serve well, but carvers generally prefer a mallet with square head, or one the shape of a wooden potato masher. I prefer a head shaped like the frustum of a cone, with the handle inserted in a hole in the smaller base. A boxwood head is to be avoided as it chips badly under continued pounding.

CHAPTER III

CARVING IN LOW RELIEF

A SURFACE of wood may be decorated by cutting
away certain portions of it, as every boy knows who
does work with a jig saw. It is not necessary, however,
to pierce the wood entirely through, in order to produce a decorative effect, as a slight sinking of the
surface suffices to throw the design into relief, and a
few added furrows incised into the surface with the
veining tool will add lines and accents needed to make
the design complete and effective. This simple kind
of decoration was employed by the Norman, the Ori-
ental and the Tyrolean wood-carvers, and our early
American furniture builders carved panels in this manner for their chests and cupboards.

Fig. 9 shows a carved panel, called a "tulip pattern,"
drawn for a Connecticut chest made about 1650. In
the original, the flat surface is painted a different color
from the background in order to heighten the effect of
the relief. Another pattern, Fig. 10, was taken from
an old chest, said to have "come over in the *May-
flower*." The design is made up of S-shaped forms

23

repeated in every possible position. I made use of this in carving a mantelpiece so situated that the light must fall full upon it, precluding the use of relief orna-

Fig. 9   Fig. 10

ment. Instead of using color contrast to strengthen the effect, I stippled the background with a punch, mottling and darkening it.

The student should try carving this design, making it, like the original, 10¾ inches long, 4 inches wide, the carving only ⅛ inch deep. It will give him much experience in choosing gouges with sweeps fitting the various curves, and the sharp angles will exercise him in the use of the bent chisels.

In Europe this shallow carving was applied to elaborate designs including plants, animals and stately men and women. There are coffers thus embellished in the Museums of London and Paris. In those examples the flat surface of the wood seemed to the designer to lack richness and to fail in telling its story, so he added shallow lines and patterns with various punches to indicate draperies and varying surface textures.

Carving like that just described is too much like embroidery to satisfy the true wood-carver who finds his greatest joy in making the chips fly. Even the slight relief given to interlacing ribbons will content the carver more, both in the result and in the doing. Intricate patterns of this sort were carved in stone at an early date, and are to be seen at Rome, Ravenna and Venice. They seem to have been copied by the wood-carvers of Scandinavia; for in the northern lands the churches, houses and even the ships were embellished with carvings in this manner (see Head-Piece of this chapter).

A simple, interlacing design is given in Fig. 11. A and B shown in two stages of development. Draw the design on the wood with a pencil and compass, then choose shallow gouges which just fit the curves of the ribbon and stop-cut the portions which are to be sunken, taking great care not to cut across the ribbon. Slice away the background to a depth of ⅛ inch or less, smoothing it down with a firmer chisel in the usual way. The pattern now appears as shown in A, as if done with a jig saw and glued to the block, but seems lifeless and lacking in charm. Now make one ribbon seem to cross over another, rising, dipping and rising again, as if it were twisted and braided into a knotted rosette. This we accomplish by stop-cutting and slicing downward a thin wedge from a ribbon which is to pass under another. The over-and-under

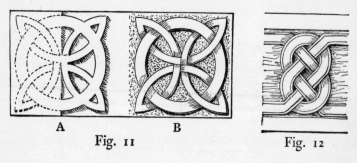

A   B

Fig. 11   Fig. 12

movement is easily followed in B, Fig. 11, and the slices which produce the effect are clearly indicated. The background may then be stippled as shown in the drawing.

A most interesting running design is formed from two parallel ribbons, which, at certain regular intervals loop and interlace with each other, forming knots like the figure 8 as shown in Fig. 12; B, sliced so as to undulate and under-pass. The movement and the interlacing can be accentuated by running narrow grooves near the edges of the ribbons, as shown at C, Fig. 12. When the ribbons are slightly hollowed in the middle they are called "straps" and the carving so treated, "strapwork." In France this strapwork was extensively carved as a decoration for panels, where considerable flat ground was left plain, and the straps were given curves more sweeping and graceful, consequently more restful.

In practicing strapwork the pupil should take an exercise in carving a running pattern frequently to be seen in wood-carving of the seventeenth century, called the "guilloche," shown in Fig. 13-A. The pattern is said to have originated in Assyria, was made more elaborate by the Greeks, and appears in Roman mosaics. Lombard sculptors used a form of the guilloche to frame in and unite their medallions; an old chest in Will Shakespeare's house has the guilloche carved upon it, and at Versailles it embellishes some of the carved doors. These examples prove the sustained popularity of the pattern through many centuries of time.

It is best to lay out the design accurately on paper before drawing it on the wood, to be sure that it fills the proper space satisfactorily. Draw the central line, divide the length into an even number of equal parts, and mark the 2nd, 4th, 6th points, etc., as centers of circles. Draw the pearls of a diameter equal to half the distance from center to center, and draw the outer circles so that they are tangent to a pearl on either side. If the pattern now seems too wide for the space to be decorated, we must begin all over again, making more divisions and smaller circles; if, on the other hand, it is found to be too narrow, less divisions and larger cir-

cles must be made. The design once established may
be transferred to the wood by merely pricking the
centers through onto the center line, and drawing
the larger and the smaller circles with the compass,
taking care, however, to stop the arcs where one ribbon passes under the other, lest we cut into an upper

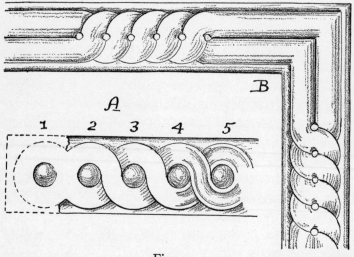

Fig. 13

ribbon in the excitement of carving. No. 1, Fig. 13,
shows the two circles in dotted lines as drawn on the
wood; 2 shows the pearl carved and the background
sunken to about 3/16 inch; 3 shows the wedge-shaped
slices taken out to a depth of ⅛ inch; 4 shows the
border furrows along the edges; and 5, the strap
scooped out all along the middle. If the pearls are
made much larger in proportion to the narrow strap,
they may be replaced by rosettes or flowers, giving

an exceedingly rich effect. Also, pearls in small circles and rosettes in larger ones, alternating with one another and bound together with narrow straps intertwined, add another variation to the possibilities of this most satisfactory motive.

Another modification of the guilloche is produced by reducing the pearls to about ⅛ inch, and making the straps very wide. The motive, too many times repeated, becomes monotonous, so the old-time designers used a group of them, about six times repeated, then allowed the straps to run along close together and parallel, separated from one another only by a ridge, till, after a tranquil interval, they were again twisted. B, Fig. 13, is copied from an oak chest from France now in my study, dating from about 1700, and I have found the same pattern carved on pieces of our early American furniture, Fig. 20, of about the same date. The pattern would look exceedingly well applied to a picture frame, the corner turn, as shown.

The slight modulations given to the strap carving introduce us to carving in high relief, a distinct advance in our craftsmanship.

Chip Carving, also called Notch Carving or Frisian Carving, should here be described, as it is a shallow surface decoration. In building my house, I designed a mantelpiece for the living room similar to one in an old French château, where the only decorative feature is a band of carving made up of incised triangles, spaced and alternating in such a manner as to give the effect of a zigzag line, Fig. 14. C. This simple decoration is often to be found on the arches of Norman churches. I marked out the design upon the wood and asked the carpenter to cut it. This he declined to attempt, saying the work was wood-carving, and he had had no experience in that craft. Though the man was a clever joiner, capable of shaping wood into any desired form, he was frightened by the name of wood-carving and dared not attempt to cut these simple triangles, so, with firmer chisels, a mallet and the co-

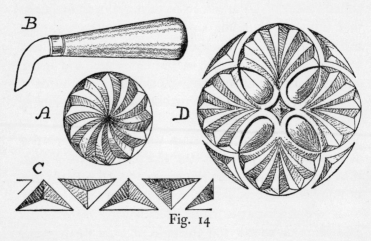

Fig. 14

operation of my two schoolboys, we quickly did the work ourselves.

As explained in carving our star, which is an example of chip carving, every triangle must first be separated into three portions by stop-cuts, deep in the center, and radiating to each apex; then triangular chips are sliced out from each edge, sloping downward and inward to the center.

Designs for chip carving are made up of triangles, either straight or curved, and cunningly arranged in

groups so as to produce some interesting pattern. At
A is shown how a circle can be treated in chip carving. The work may be executed with the usual carving tools, the carver's knife being of the greatest value
where straight-line triangles are to be carved. When
curved triangles occur, we must use gouges, or pro-
cure a special knife having the blade bent and curved
as shown at B. If a knife of this shape cannot be obtained from the dealer, it can be made from an ordinary
shoe knife, by grinding the blade to the shape shown
and sharpening the edge keenly. This knife can execute
cuts beyond the capacity of the jackknife, and is the
only tool actually necessary in chip carving, since it
can make the inner stop-cuts as well as the sloping
slices, both straight and curved.

The entire interest in chip carving resides in the
cleanness of the cuts and the sharpness of the edges.
It is, therefore, desirable to choose a wood of a texture
as homogeneous as possible, and we would suggest
black walnut, cypress, maple or mahogany for the purpose, discarding oak and chestnut because their grains
are variable in texture and resistance. A sharp tool and
a bold cut should leave a shiny, almost polished surface. An elaborate design, suitable for chip carving
is given at D, Fig. 14.

CHAPTER IV

CARVING IN HIGH RELIEF

SHALLOW carvings combined with flat surfaces and sunken grounds are effective decorations, but they lack the charm and refinement, the grace and varying play of light and shade obtainable in rounded forms and changing planes.

The flat carving needs to be rounded off or sloped, to make it more interesting, but the rounding and sloping must be done thoughtfully, tastefully, and with definite purpose. This work is called "modeling," a term borrowed from the sculptor who models in clay, and quite appropriately, since the carver *is* a sculptor whose work is only less highly esteemed than that of the sculptor in marble and bronze. Modeling, it should be explained, is not merely rounding off the edges of a flat surface, or scooping out a hollow. Modeling means a shaping and modulation of the form to suggest some object in nature, or to produce an artistic effect.

To illustrate what I mean, recall that a sphere, an egg, an apple and a grape, each has its individual form, although all are round, solid objects. Also, place a rose petal, a seashell and a spoon side by side, and notice that these hollow forms have subtle curvatures, differing one from the other. A leaf of rhubarb presents a surface made up of many undulations and depressions, varying in height, shape and curvature, illustrating admirably what is meant by "modeling." But though I refer to natural forms to explain the meaning of the term, I want it understood that we are never to copy nature, for ours is a decorative art, which aims only to catch the spirit of natural forms, and interpret their grace and charm.

If possible, the student should examine some of the specimens of wood carving to be found in the museum, and especially in the English room and the Morgan Collection of the Metropolitan Museum, New York, and note how plants, flowers and fruits are rendered by the master carvers of the olden times. In my drawing of the French carving at the head of Chapter I, I have endeavored to show how the vine leaves are modeled, how they rise and fall, how leaves lap over one another and seem to clasp the stems. Flower petals are modeled in such a way as to catch the light at various angles, and stems wave and twist in harmonious curves, the whole design giving the feeling of a living, growing thing, without exactly copying any vine that ever grew.

An exercise in modeling to interpret natural form is found in the panel shown on the left in Fig. 15. An oak leaf, natural size, was chosen as the decorative motive, repeated four times around the center, the tips filling the angles of the panel, and the stems making a whirling cross at the center. At A the outline on the wood is shown in dotted lines, at B the sunken ground is cut away, at C the leaf is modeled in undulations suggested by the natural leaf, keeping all the outer edges high, but scooping the interior down more or less toward the veins. At D the veins are given relief by deep cuts on either side with the veining tool. All the outer edges of the leaves are on a level with the original surface of the panel, and the midrib valley is the deepest, but never so deep as the ground. The valleys of the side veins are shallow at

Fig. 15

the tips, but slope down to join the midrib, while the sections between veins are higher at the curved indentations, rounding down into the adjacent valleys like watersheds between neighboring rivers.

The other square panel in Fig. 15 to the right of that with oak leaves, will give us more advanced practice in modeling. The figure represents a panel twelve inches square, the original of which is in the Victoria and Albert Museum in London, recently copied in butternut wood to embellish my studio doors. The panel is divided into four small squares, in each of which is a heart-shaped pattern, enclosing a shell. The four hearts, which form a bold outline like a four-leaf clover, are clearly distinguished from surrounding embellishments. Each shell is beautifully modeled, swelling at the base, sinking down and rising again to the margin, in an elegant manner, as indicated in the sectional diagram I. The flame-shaped forms inside the hearts, and the eight little ornaments filling corners and empty spaces, all give opportunity for modeling.

The different steps of carving are clearly indicated in the drawing: at E the pattern is shown in dotted lines on the wood, where details of the shell are omitted, because the wood surface is there to be cut away; at F the ground is sunken to the boundaries of the pattern, at G the flames are outlined, and the shell is carefully modeled, as a smooth and sweeping curved surface, unbroken by the furrows and cuts which are to suggest flutings, likewise postponing the indication of the pearls. A template, J, of cardboard or tin should be cut out to the exact required curvature of the shell, I, with which to test the correctness of our carving as it proceeds. The first cut into the shell should be a deep curved trench cut with the ⅜ inch gouge, forming a quarter-circle through the point G, going down as deep as the deepest part of the shell is to be. This quarter-circle will serve as a stop-cut for all the slicing out of the shell, as thus we can safely slice down into it from any direction. While the slicing proceeds frequent tests must be made with the template in positions radial to the shell, to make sure that the curved surface is developing properly, for upon the graceful swelling, sinking and rising of this surface, depends the charm of the shell composition. I dwell upon this matter for the reason that it is our first study, leading to the analysis and rendering of curved forms in general. I have been amazed to discover that many cultivated people are unaware of the distinction between concave and convex forms, and purblind to the beauty embodied in subtle relief forms which occur in carving, sculpture, silverwork, countless examples of which are to be found in nature.

Wood-carving pursued as a hobby will cultivate in the student a faculty for observing these subtle distinctions of form in nature and also add greatly to his enjoyment of beautiful things in art. With heightened appreciation he will visit the museums of antiques, and also treasure more fondly any well-designed object of his own. Moreover, when the opportunity comes to him to visit Europe, he will have advantage over his fellow travelers in discovering greater sympathy with the master craftsmen of the olden times and understanding of their work.

To pursue successfully the work of modeling in relief, and to carry it to a degree of real refinement, the student should resort to actual modeling in some plastic material like clay or plasticine. I do not mean to suggest that he is to work in an art school from the human model, but merely that he should try out the motives he intends to carve by building them up and shaping their surfaces in relief until he is satisfied with the depth and contour of every part.

Curves found in nature are rarely arcs of circles,

and our appreciation of subtle forms is derived, first-
hand, from natural growths, and secondly from works
of art. The stems of orchids and the fronds of ferns
are examples in nature, as are the profiles of Doric
columns and contours of Greek vases in the realm of
art. If the wood-carver has a feeling for these refine-
ments of form, he can interpret them with his dexterous hand, and this in turn will react upon his mind,

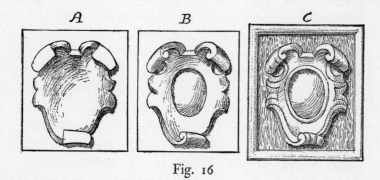

Fig. 16

making his observation more keen, his taste more
critical.

An exercise should now be made in carving in bold
relief, for which I have chosen an example of antique
carving from an old chest I bought in Italy many
years ago. The original is a panel of Italian walnut
about six inches square framed in by a moulding. In
Fig. 16 I have shown the design called "cartouche" in
three progressive stages of carving. We must choose
a piece of wood amply thick to allow for deep carving, and large enough to allow the edges to be covered
by the moulding. We trace the pattern on the face of

the block, and all around the edges of the same we draw a sharp pencil line to indicate the depth to cut the ground. We then free the central motive of wood down to this line, and smooth the ground, and, leaving in the rough the three projections where the edges are to roll over, we hollow out the shield in a smooth and graceful sweep, as shown in A. To accomplish this, we dig a sort of well down the middle, to the depth of the hollow shield, and slice downward into it from all sides, clearing away the wood with bold strokes, then gradually refining the surface with careful slicing till the desired form is attained. Now we trace the outline of the egg-shaped depression, and sink it as shown in B, treating it exactly as if it were a big "pearl." Next, the three uncut blocks may be shaped into cylinders on the front sides, while their backs are made to curl, as seen in the sketch.

We see in C the finishing touches added with the veining tool, and the edge of the egg-shaped opening gracefully rounded off. The panel gains in effect when framed by the moulding.

This exercise has been chosen to illustrate an important problem which often presents itself in high-relief carving, namely, how to render forms at different depths.

In such cases, as in the cartouche just completed, it is best to carve and model the shallower surface, without regard to the deeper digging that is to follow, and when this is satisfactorily accomplished to trace upon it the outline of the form on the lower level, proceeding then to carve and model that as a second stage. If we sink our ground deep enough, we shall cut entirely through the wood, and thus arrive at what is called *pierced carving*.

This is a form of jigsaw work carried to a higher degree of refinement. Patterns for pierced carving must be made so that the wood connects and is self-supporting, and the wood should be sufficiently strong and tough to endure the work of carving, as well as to withstand the numberless accidents it may experience in the future.

Fig. 17

Copying our design on the wood, we cut out all the openings as accurately as possible with the jigsaw, then fasten the work with brads at the corners to a thick, flat board of the same size, to give support to the delicate filigree of wood while we carve. We are in constant danger of breaking our work, so must proceed with careful, delicate slices, yet never niggling.

Pierced carvings have their uses in panels of doors where ventilation is desirable. In many old English churches we find the door between chancel and sacristy furnished with pierced panels called "squints," to prevent collisions between persons passing in opposite directions. I find that squints are desirable in doors dividing a dining room from a butler's pantry, and have designed and carved a number of them, shown in Fig. 17. In planning these small designs, we are free to choose any quaint or grotesque motive such as a dog, a fish or a dolphin. The central design was to be placed in the door of the telephone closet, to show whether the instrument was in use or not, and the motive chosen was appropriately a parrot! The squint was backed with glass to insulate the sound of conversation, while giving a view of the interior. Pierced carvings occur frequently as portions of Gothic work, as we shall find in studying carvings of that period.

CHAPTER V

WOODS SUITABLE TO CARVE

I HAVE postponed dealing with the matter of woods to carve, assuming that the student would try his tools and gain a certain amount of experience in experimenting with pieces of wood he found at hand, just as I did in the beginning.

Thus trying and discovering that wood-carving was fun, I also discovered that I must choose my wood according to the furniture I wished to build and then fit my pattern and mode of treatment to the space and the circumstances. A goodly number of woods were at once stricken from the available list: lignum vitæ, ebony, boxwood and white oak because of their extreme hardness; apple and pear wood because large enough pieces are not available; yellow southern pine because it splinters badly and is full of resin; fir, spruce and hemlock because they are woods employed for purposes where carved decorations would be inappropriate.

Of woods useful for carving, the most extensively used in the past is oak. The thousands of choir stalls in the cathedrals and the acres of rich wainscot in old castle halls are of oak. But we must distinguish between European oak and our own. The former seems tighter, more homogeneous, yet softer than ours.

American white oak should be avoided, because it is too hard to carve with any degree of pleasure or satisfaction. But red oak, black oak and rock oak have not this objection. They can be carved quite readily, yet have sufficient hardness to resist wear and hard usage. Therefore, furniture of a sturdy type, chairs, dining tables, blanket chests, wood boxes, should be made from one of these latter, and because they are rather coarse of grain, ornaments should be in bold design, frankly carved with clean, deep cuts, and a studied disregard of finish.

I should recommend a study of some of the antique pieces in the museums for an understanding of this matter of *neat unfinish*, of frank rendering of essential forms. The grain of red oak is somewhat coarse and the carving is necessarily crude, and at times clumsy, but you will appreciate that the rugged workmanship gives to the exhibit an air that is in keeping with its style and purpose. Sturdy peasants of Normandy and hard-headed Puritan settlers liked to have their linen chests and their cupboards strong like themselves, with but little of the graces and elegances of a later time. The furniture of French or Italian walnut, often mistaken for oak, takes more refined embellishments with higher finish.

Chestnut is a most valuable wood, though now difficult to obtain, because of the destructive ravages of the chestnut blight. The grain may be so chosen as to present beautiful figures in the plain, uncarved portions, while sections to be carved may be cut where grain is less conspicuous. In carving chestnut wood.

the craftsman needs to use caution because the hard layers are interspersed with softer ones. Cutting from the former into the latter, the tool is apt to make a sudden jump, and often may do harm. Any scooping motion of the tool may catch and lift a hard chip away from the softer stratum below it.

The cross-section of a tree trunk exhibits a series of rings of woody fiber separated by rings of softer cellular tissue, and from the center outward radial plates of tissue, called "medullary rays," are observed. In oak and chestnut the hard and soft tissues are strongly pronounced, and they are disposed to dry, or "season," with unequal rapidity. The result of this is that if a trunk is sawed into parallel boards the full width of the tree trunk, they have a tendency to split or warp in drying.

A remedy for this has been found in what is known as "quartering." This is done as follows: three or four boards are sawed out of the center of the log, the full width, then the two remaining outside segments are cut down the middle, making four "quarters." These are then sliced into four boards, given a quarter turn and again sliced at right angles to the previous cuts. Quartering gives rise to more waste of wood, and produces many narrow boards, but it has the advantage that the boards, cut more nearly radially, are less likely to warp and split in course of seasoning, and in addition to this, cuts through the medullary rays present an agreeable pattern called a "figure," by which we can always recognize quartered wood.

The American black walnut is fine for carving, because of its firm, even grain. The purplish-brown tint of the raw wood takes on a richness and depth of tone when waxed or varnished, making it particularly desirable for any kind of furniture or interior finish. Back in the eighties the biggest and best of our grand black walnut trees were felled and made up into suites of furniture, pretentious in aspect and detestable in design, with extra ornaments glued on here and there to heighten the ostentatious effect. Occasionally antiques from those Dark Ages can be bought at a low price and their splendid wood can be worked into new productions. The supply of new wood to be had from dealers is excellent but generally sold in narrow stock.

Mahogany is more extensively used for furniture and cabinetwork than any other wood, and for the reason that it has strength, beauty of marking, richness of color and is excellent to carve. All mahogany is imported, the best coming from Honduras and Mexico. Trees growing in moist ground produce a soft, coarse wood, light in weight, while those from rocky, elevated positions, though smaller in size, give a wood harder and more beautifully veined. Spanish and African mahogany are inferior. Huge logs four or five feet in diameter, and sometimes fifty feet long, are cut and dragged out of the tropical forests and shipped, often as ballast. Duncan Phyfe, the famous cabinetmaker, was known to the sea captains arriving at the port of New York as a craftsman ever ready to purchase the finest logs of mahogany, and they were in the habit of giving him the first choice of their precious cargo.

The rich, dark mahogany from which Early American furniture was made is three times as heavy as that now obtainable, one square foot of it weighing as much as six pounds. A leaf from an extension table some sixty years old has given me a number of choice bits, taking the finest patterns and rewarding the most dexterous of efforts.

It is said that mahogany was first used in 1595 to repair ships of the fleet of Sir Walter Raleigh, but was obtainable in London only in 1720 when a cabinet-maker recognized its valuable qualities.

Chippendale, Heppelwhite and Sheraton made use of it with great elegance, but added carved embellishments with much reserve. In France, however, the simple beauty of mahogany was eclipsed by the application of ornate trimmings of brass, fire gilt, known as ormulu. Lacking these brass ornaments, the American wood-carver was content to copy their decorative effect in his wood.

The French furniture made about 1800 and spoken of as Empire style, was almost exclusively of mahogany, and richly carved with dragons, griffins, pineapples and acanthus leaves, and from this source much of our Early American furniture derived its inspiration.

Cherry wood, though hard to carve, takes clear, sharp cuts and resists hard usage. A less precious wood than mahogany, it was used for humble purposes, but under a rich stain it often masquerades as the former.

The woods next to be mentioned are less adapted to fine furniture, but fill many a useful purpose.

Maple is firm and hard. Whitewood, derived from a certain poplar tree, is softer than maple, but excellent to carve. A peculiarity must be noted, that a board presents two distinct qualities and colors: the portion which formed the heart of the tree is greenish in tint and hard; the portion called the "sap," which grew near the bark, is white and soft. Tulip wood is sometimes called whitewood.

Basswood comes from the linden tree called in England the lime tree. It has a slightly brownish tint and is softer than whitewood, but the fiber is less brittle. Slivers made from it bend without breaking, and thin panels may be steamed and easily bent into cylindrical shapes.

Butternut is soft and homogeneous, and therefore delightful to carve, but should be employed only where it is protected from hard usage. The same may be said of white pine and cypress.

Red cedar is attractive because of its agreeable color and odor, but since it is to be had only in narrow stock, its use is restricted to the making of small articles. It takes a sharp, clear cut, and is particularly suited for chip carving.

Sweet gum wood, also known as satinwood, has a smooth and uniform texture, excellent for carving, yet sufficiently firm to make durable furniture. The brownish color becomes richer when varnished.

California redwood has a superb red color but an exceedingly soft texture; too much so for general use in furniture building, but delightful to carve. Since so many other woods are available, it would seem both

wise and patriotic to leave the majestic redwood se-
quoias where they have been growing since the time
of the Pharaohs, to stand as great national monu-
ments, rather than to sacrifice them to the passing needs
of today.

In ordering wood for carving from a carpenter or
a supply house, we should specify that it is to be
planed, face and back, to the exact thickness required,
but that plenty of allowance should be made in
length and width of every piece for necessary fitting
or for possible changes in design. It is helpful in placing our design on the wood to have an extra inch to
spare, a surplus easily removed in making up the finished piece.

Staining and finishing: The surface of wood,
whether carved or plain, always needs some form of
treatment, to protect it from moisture and dust, to
change its color or to bring out the beauty of its grain.

To preserve the natural appearance of bare wood,
while protecting its surface, apply one or more thin
coats of bleached shellac dissolved in denatured or
grain alcohol.

Usually we desire to change the color of the wood,
using a penetrative stain whose medium is water, alcohol or varnish. Wood stain is a dye, not a paint, and
it should be made from analine dyes or vegetable coloring matter, not from paints having a heavy, earthy
body which will not penetrate. Stains of many tints
are sold ready for use, with explicit directions for applying them, and only a few suggestions are needed

here. Make sure that the wood surface is free from grease and any spots of glue, as stains cannot penetrate them. Try your stain upon a sample of wood of the kind used in carving, and let it dry, to make sure the shade is not too dark, for it is much better to arrive at the tint with several applications; it is almost impossible to lighten a stain once applied. The effect of relief may be increased upon carving by staining the whole, then quickly wiping the surface and highlights, while leaving the background and deep cuts to dry a darker tone.

When the stain is thoroughly dry, give the wood surface a coat of orange shellac. When purchased ready for use this is usually thick like heavy cream, and should be thinned with alcohol to the consistency of skimmed milk, so as to leave no shine upon the wood.

Lastly, apply several coats of prepared wax, rubbing each coat and allowing it to dry before the next is applied. This wax finish gives an agreeable satin luster without a glossy shine, and is found excellent for oak, chestnut and walnut.

It is scarcely likely that the craftsman will desire to varnish his carved wood. If varnish is used upon mahogany furniture, it must be applied to the highly finished carving as well as to the flat surfaces, but the dull finish for the entire piece seems more agreeable, and assuredly no craftsman wants his oak or walnut to be cheapened with a shiny varnish. When desired, however, varnishes are to be had in great variety, and each presents its own fussy peculiarities. The title of a valuable little book on the subject is given in our list of books of reference at the end of this volume.

Lastly, let me repeat a caution already given: order your wood planed and scraped, but *never* sandpapered.

CHAPTER VI

DESIGNS FOR WOOD-CARVING

THE question often arises as to what to carve and how to get designs. For a time one does well to follow the traditional method, and derive patterns from excellent work of earlier times, keeping in mind, however, that the motive chosen is a flexible, plastic thing to expand, modify and apply to suit one's own needs, and to carve in a way to make it harmonize with the whole work in hand.

Let me describe the stages in the production of a piece of carved furniture, to illustrate the evolution of a design. I wished to replace an old and ugly bookcase belonging to the "black walnut period" with a more pleasing bookshelf in chestnut, and made my drawing of the upper part to scale, as shown at A, Fig. 18. The width of the space to be filled was 47 inches, which would be that of the new piece. The total height was fixed at 5 feet 1½ inches to correspond to that of the mantelshelf near by, and the depth of the shelves 9½ inches. Elevating the lower shelf 4½ inches from the floor, and surrounding it with a baseboard, I spaced the shelves 10, 9, 9 and 8 inches, respectively, one above another. The upper portion remaining to be dealt with measured 47 inches wide and 18¾ high, and in this I planned to construct

50

a cabinet, closed with carved doors, and overhanging
the lower shelves by two inches.

Making all allowances for the width of structural
parts, I arrived at the following dimensions of the
parts to be carved: Each cabinet door, 13½ inches
wide and 11¾ high, the central panel 5½ inches wide
and 11¾ high, the running pattern above, 40 inches
long and only 1 inch high, the panels in each side of

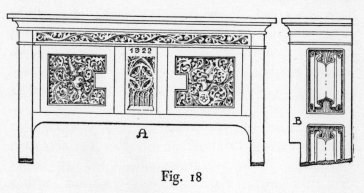

Fig. 18

the bookcase figured out 5½ inches wide by 9 inches
high.

This form of bookcase, surmounted with an overhanging, closed cupboard, suggested a piece of Gothic
furniture called a "credenza" or "credence table," a
favorite with cabinetmakers of the fifteenth century;
accordingly I sought designs for carving in harmony
with works of that period. For the doors I found an
elaborate armorial pattern consisting of a crested shield
surmounted by a helmet. Upon this latter was a "mantle" cut and slashed into ribbons, and flying out in
restless curves in every direction till it entirely filled

the panel with intricate pattern, shown at A. The same pattern, turned over and repeated on the opposite door-panel produced bilateral symmetry desirable in such cases.

The upright, central panel suggested a narrow Gothic window design and was readily filled with a pointed arch enclosing a rose window, with five small arches below.

There remained the horizontal member above the doors to be decorated, for which I chose a design from an old English church. With so much ornament on the front of the bookcase, it was hardly fair to starve the upright sides. The former being of Gothic design, the latter must be of the same style, so the best motive for the purpose seemed to be the "parchment fold," and this was introduced as shown in the drawing at B, Fig. 18.

I do not wish to give the impression that the work of designing went forward without changes. On the contrary, excepting for the height and width, all dimensions were changed over and over again. Everything is a matter of "trial and error," all proportions must be considered as tentative, and the design as plastic, till all points have been considered, and have been given their due preponderance. Only when the structural plan has been fully established may we determine the size of our carving patterns, and it is well to have cabinetwork started, and panels and members cut to fit, before the design for carving is drawn on the wood.

I found all these appropriate Gothic designs as illustrations in books on old furniture, but all of them on a greatly reduced scale, so my first duty consisted in enlarging the designs and adjusting them to fit my spaces to be decorated. Laying out accurately these spaces on paper, I proceeded to sketch in the important features, the helmet, the shield, the curves of the mantle, etc., rubbing out, shifting, adjusting the details till the entire design seemed to cover and decorate its allotted space in a satisfactory manner. The next step was to transfer this pattern to the wood, a process usually accomplished by means of carbon paper. The latter is laid upon the wood, the pattern pinned upon it with thumb tacks so as not to slip, and every line followed with even pressure with the point of a hard pencil, though in place of a pencil point I prefer to use a knitting needle mounted in a wooden handle, as this does not leave marks upon the paper in following the line. In pinning down the pattern, I take pains to place the thumb tacks where the holes they make will eventually disappear in carving.

I am well aware that not every pupil has had the experience to enable him to enlarge and work out an elaborate pattern, free-hand, so I will suggest other ways to accomplish the same end.

There is a little machine called a "pantograph" with which we may copy and enlarge a design; also, a more accurate instrument called a "reflectograph" based on the principle of the camera lucida, which we can buy from an optician. A much used method is called "enlarging by squares," shown in Fig. 19. Take a piece

of transparent paper, like the so-called onionskin tracing paper, or a piece of cellophane; rule it with pen
and ink accurately into a large number of small squares.
Lay this over the design to be copied and note the
number of squares in width and height which cover
the subject. Then draw on paper the full size of your
proposed carving, divide this up into exactly the same
number of squares as previously noted, then copy the
design, square by square, working it out as if it were
a piece of needlework. Make necessary corrections

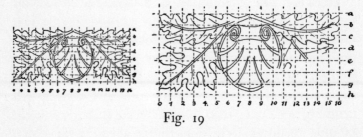

Fig. 19

with eraser and pencil, ink in the lines and transfer
to the wood in the usual manner.

A design of any sort may be photographed, a lantern slide made from it, and the image thrown on
paper with a lantern; the image may then be accurately
limned. Large public libraries are equipped to furnish
photostat enlargements of pictures and designs found
in their books. If the design is already a relief carved
in wood or sculptured in stone, a crude copy may be
made on stout paper by laying this over it and rubbing
with a soft pencil. Enough of the outline will catch
the lead to permit of filling out with the pen; but
rubbing will not give an enlarged pattern.

All these schemes for copying and enlarging are but "dodges" to avoid drawing the pattern free-hand, and it is to be hoped that the hobby of wood-carving may be an inducement for the pupil to cultivate the power to draw. At school most of us have been taught to put down on paper, with a lead pencil, free-hand, the shapes of objects set before us. The power thus acquired makes it possible to copy our designs from carvings we like, from illustrations in books, or from the myriad beautiful forms found in nature.

Drawing, like writing, is but a means of recording our thoughts. Consider that the cave dwellers, whose civilization was most primitive, acquired such skill in drawing that they were able to depict the reindeer, buffalo, bears and many creatures now extinct on the walls of their caverns. Surely, we of the twentieth century, with our facilities and our instruction, should be able to do as well as primitive men in the dawn of civilization. If we can draw even a little, we can make use of original material for designs, as such material lies about us in abundance. Our native flora provides us with leaf forms and flower forms; butterflies, reptiles and fishes are decorative; fruits, cones and seed vessels may be employed; snow crystals and frost on the windowpane, branches against the sky, seaweeds on the shore, all furnish material from which motives may be chosen for our purpose.

But Nature does not compose patterns. Her laws are not the laws of design. A realistic and pretty sketch is not sufficient for our work. In examining good decorative works, we discover they are not copies of nature, but are built upon laws of their own, chief of which are the laws of balance and of repetition. I must not attempt to explain all about decorative design, but believe it will be useful to the wood-carver to know the two main principles. A design is balanced if there is as much decoration in one portion as in another, or, where divided in the middle, the motive on the right is turned over and repeated on the left, this is called "bilateral symmetry." A circle may be decorated in this manner, or it may be divided into radial sectors, or into annular zones, and these divisions decorated with a repeated motive. If a motive is copied again and again, as in chintz or wall paper, a decorative effect is produced, as we saw in the moulding over the doors of our bookcase in Fig. 18. A square may be divided into four smaller squares and decorated by four repetitions, as we saw in the panels in Fig. 15.

Now we will take as an example of original material applied to wood-carving a box we made to house our yule log, to preserve it from one Christmas to another. A perspective view of this box in outline is shown at A, Fig. 20. The front and each end presented rectangles to be decorated, the ends of the arched lid two low lunettes, and the lid a rectangular curved surface. Circles were introduced in the rectangles, two in front for inscriptions, two on the ends to receive wheel-patterns. Yuletide symbols of holly and mistletoe were appropriate and no great ingenuity was needed to fill the little spaces and the lunettes with sprigs of these plants, nor to make wheels out of holly leaves with holly berries bunched in the center, as seen at B and C.

For the domestic ceremony of the yule log, flames
of fire were appropriate, therefore, a design made up
of flaming tongues was applied to the lid, at D, leaving
a space in the center for a tablet on which to carve
the lines of a poem. In this whole design perfect

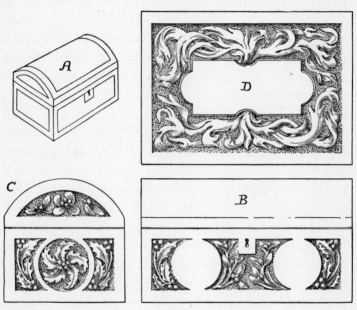

Fig. 20

balance and frequent repetition are to be noted. Circles
and branches are repeated at either side of the center
line, and the flames are repeated in opposite corners.

If we find that we are not able to draw the plant
or flower we want for our motive, we may sometimes
trace it, as I did in the case of the oak leaves, in Fig.
15, or cast the shadow upon a piece of blueprint paper,

and get a shadow print to use and repeat as desired. Most motives used in decorations are derived from forms in nature, but there are many abstruse forms

Fig. 21

quite as applicable to the purpose. The circle is a most useful decorative unit. Moorish artists, forbidden by the laws of the Mohammedan religion to use natural forms, made excellent use of many-sided polygons and straight lines, binding and interweaving them in intricate and interesting patterns. I knew a Yale professor of mathematics who plotted a complex curve from an algebraic formula, had it printed in outline of gilt, and by repetition made of it an excellent and original wall paper for his entrance hall. A lady living in our part of the country, who makes hooked rugs, obtains her patterns by folding a newspaper up-and-down and crosswise, cuts odd-shaped, curvilinear holes through them, and opens them out, developing a pattern of perfect symmetry and balance, one motive being four times repeated around the center. She then weaves her rugs from this pattern. These instances demonstrate that any motive, properly repeated, will produce a decorative design, leaving out all question of drawing or of art.

But there may be such a thing as decoration without formal balance. The Japanese are masters of decoration whose work, without being pictorial, departs from the rigid rules. Following a similar plan, a sketch from nature, a native iris flower, shown on the left of Fig. 21, is applied to a narrow, upright panel, on the right, a few changes made in the leaves and the buds, and the empty space of the upper right hand decorated with a dragon fly. In carving a naturalistic subject like this, one should keep the work as purely decorative as possible, and resist any temptation to indulge in pictorial realism.

CHAPTER VII

TECHNIQUE AND FINISH

WHEN we have learned to make a design and to carve it to our taste, we find ourselves confronted by two questions: How much ornament shall we plan for our work? Where shall we apply it for the best effect?

Many valuable pieces of antique carved furniture to be seen in the museums are covered with an excess of carved ornaments, and in the cathedrals of Europe we find the choirs generally filled with woodwork too exuberant in its embellishment. The guide books are likely to praise all such works without reserve, but we should keep to our own standards of taste and judge all such works for ourselves, according to their simplicity of design and excellence in execution. Where the structural lines are obscured and all the surfaces are covered with patterns we may be sure that the carver has done too much. A good rule to follow is to restrict carved ornament to one third of the surface of any member of furniture; its effect thus will be enhanced by contrast with the plain, undecorated portions surrounding it.

The structure is more important than the ornament, and it should be emphasized rather than obscured by the design worked upon it. If the framework is carved, the panels should be left plain, or vice versa. To carve both frame and panels is to overdecorate the whole and diminish its beauty.

A panel should always be treated as a *panel*, with decoration sunken more or less below its surface, never protruding from it. Buffets and wardrobes are often manufactured with doors bearing lumpy carvings on their panels representing game or fruit or fishes, done in the highest possible relief, and to make them more real they are frequently undercut so as to seem hanging free in front of the background. Too often the motive is carved as a separate piece, and is glued on, masquerading as part of the panel. The deceit is likely to be unmasked, however, by the failure of the glue to hold.

Redundancy of ornament fatigues rather than delights the eye of the observer, and for practical reasons also the carving should be restrained. A chair-back should never be made uncomfortable by carved embellishments, nor should excrescences be left to catch the clothing or the dust. It is sufficient to carve the upper panels of a door, leaving the lower ones plain, and in the case of a wainscoted room, the upper panels are the only ones needing ornament.

Having settled upon our design and its location, we need now to know how best to carve it, since by the study of old work we have learned that there are many ways of "treating" or "rendering" a given subject, just as we may express the same thought in many different languages.

There is much wood-carving made by machinery,

geometrically and technically perfect but utterly un-
interesting. On the other hand, we often come upon
hand-carving which is labored, undercut, elaborated
to the last detail, and yet fails to attract and charm.

Between the purely mechanical work, on the one
hand, and the excessive handwork, on the other, lies
a mean course which we should discover and follow
if we are to get the full joy out of our hobby. We
must come back to the first principle that the purpose
of carving is to make a surface interesting through a
play of light and shade, and a pleasing balance of
masses, a suggestion of graceful line; all of this irre-
spective of the realistic appearance of the subject.
Then, in addition to the decoration inherent in the
design, there may be given the charm of clever
toolwork.

Every craft has its technique, founded upon the
tools and the materials. In old illuminated manuscripts
we recognize the work of the quill pen; this replaced
by the pen of steel gave us modern penmanship with
shades and flourishes. Bristle brushes and canvas with
a "tooth" produced the brushwork seen in modern
oil paintings. From these various crafts we deduce that
wood-carving must have a technique peculiarly its
own, its form of expression, its vocabulary and its
syntax.

In the first place we have to choose one of four
possible ways for treating our pattern: (1) to sink the
pattern into the surface; (2) to sink the ground and
leave the design as a flat silhouette; (3) to sink the
ground more or less deeply and carve the design in

relief, or (4) to make a pierced carving as we did in Chap. IV. An inscription may be carved in incised lettering, or by cutting away the ground and leaving the letters in relief.

The treatment of the ground is also susceptible of numerous variations, besides merely smoothing; namely, by stippling with a point or punching with

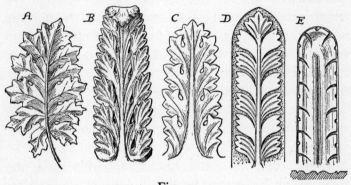

Fig. 22

a pattern, lining it with the veining tool or gouging it into uneven waves.

After this we have to decide how best to modulate the form of each decorative unit, and here we have two guides, one or the other of which we may choose to follow: the method displayed by antique examples of wood-carving or the scheme suggested by the appearance of natural objects.

As to the former, we discover that the master wood-carvers have worked out numerous shorthand methods for rendering their motives, methods we may follow for a time till we have developed our personal style.

But a motive taken direct from nature should suggest clever interpretation, not slavish copying.

To illustrate various interpretations of one motive, let us take the example of the acanthus leaf shown in Fig. 22, a favorite with sculptors since the time of the Greeks, and compare the various treatments employed in rendering it.

At A is a pencil study made in Rome from an actual leaf gathered by the roadside; B is taken from a Greek capital in marble; C, from an old Italian walnut chest; D, from an English chest; E, from a cupboard made in Normandy. Comparing these interpretations with the leaf which inspired them, we learn that for decorative purposes we need not copy minute details, we need not allow nature to "cramp our style." Every leaf, every object in nature, has a decorative character, and when this is seized and interpreted all less important details may be summarized or suppressed.

As a study in rendering an interpretation let me present the design for a box lid, Fig. 23. Each of the fruits has its characteristic outline, its well-rounded and smooth surface; the leaves are strongly modeled, with their toothed edges merely indicated; the bark of the branches is made rough and bold; the basket is interpreted in a kind of "shorthand" way, which plainly means basketwork to any observer.

It is precisely such inventions of original treatment that exercise the ingenuity of the carver and give him endless delight in his labor.

Textures call for perpetual invention and applica-

tion of skill. Drapery and hair may be epitomized in
a series of bold grooves, water indicated by undulating
curves, fur and feathers by a few sharp incisions.
When we undertake work involving the human figure,
we can venture to represent hands and feet with
Byzantine simplicity by merely indicating fingers and
toes with narrow grooves separating them. Heads
preferably should be carved in profile, modeled as

Fig. 23

simply as possible, but with features strongly char-
acterized.

To sum up the matter of treatment, let every cut
be frank and purposeful, avoid much detail and do
not seek a high finish. Let the work show that it is
the work of a sharp tool in a trained hand! Some
wood-carvers, in an excess of zeal to make their work
an exact replica of nature, go so far as to undercut
their motives. This practice has two objections: the
practical one, that it makes the wood so frail that it
is likely to break; the artistic one, that it detaches the
ornament from the wood to be ornamented. A carved

object standing away from a panel contradicts the idea of decorative carving.

Grinling Gibbons, an English wood-carver who enjoyed a great reputation under Charles II, was a great offender in the way of realistic copying and of undercutting. It was said his carving of feathers on game and scales on fishes could hardly be distinguished from real ones, and it was so aggressively clever as to absorb the entire attention of the observer, and make him forget the work while wondering at the cleverness of Grinling Gibbons.

In the same line I must mention a piece of carving at the Musée Carnavalet in Paris, reproducing a basket of flowers. It is an astounding piece of work because every flower, bud and leaf is an evident portrait of some actual model. The basket is like a hollow cage, all its orifices pierced so as to show the mass of stems carved deep within. This monument of misapplied dexterity and lavish patience serves no purpose but to show future wood-carvers what to avoid.

Most of the wood-carving we see is machine-made. The principle of the pantograph has been taken and applied to woodworking machinery with such success that twenty pieces of carving can now be executed at one time, every one exactly like the other and possessing a finish so perfect in every detail as to put to shame the work of the ablest craftsman. To quote Kipling, we may say "It is clever, but is it Art?" The reply to our question is, "The result satisfies the purchaser." Very true, yet in the finished product we feel a hidden want. We prefer the old handwork, not because it is old, but because it bears the impress of the master hand, the human touch which no machine can ever supply. Yet, because of the mass production, the machine is in danger of moulding our taste to a false ideal, and of setting up a standard of shop-finish unworthy of our imitation.

If we try to copy machine work, we ourselves become machines, and in aiming at excessive finish, we laboriously destroy the very quality we love in ancient masterpieces. In examining them we feel that the old wood-carvers found joy in working out what they had designed, and here, I believe, we have the secret of their success. Let us work as long as work is fun, but stop as soon as it becomes laborious. In this way we cease to be slaves to the machine.

But, on the other hand, should we scorn to use the machine? The grindstone, the wood plane, the brace and bit are machines, and useful ones. We can scarcely do without the power planer, the turning lathe, the jig saw or the band saw. An electric router can rough out our patterns, and save us the toil of clearing away thousands of chips. A combination plane will furnish us with mouldings having profiles of exquisite refinement. How far, then, may we avail ourselves of these modern appliances, and yet maintain the ideal of wood-carving as a form of art? The line of division is as narrow as the thinnest shaving—for the art abides upon the surface, as it is left by the master hand, when its last, thin shaving has been cut from the carving. A bronze statue is a hollow thing with a finely modeled and patined surface, an oil painting is a canvas with a surface that the painter has created, and which no human hand may molest. The wood-carving is the surface formed to the will and under the craftsmanship of the carver, the last slices make it tell the tale. All excavations and roughing out that have gone before are but preparation for the final gesture. Hence it is evident that we may use any means at our command to take away the dull, useless, expressionless material, dig down, chip away, disclose the design lying within, but make the final surface our own, moulding it to our will by our own hands.

With this understanding, we are at liberty to use any contrivance of this Machine Age to help us in the dull "roughing out," for we shall then attack the actual work of carving with keenest enthusiasm, our eyes will be fresh for close discernment, and our appreciation of forms and textures will be unfatigued by needless toil.

Previously I stated that sandpaper should be avoided because it dulls the tools, but there is an additional and far more important reason for eschewing it. The charm of carved wood lies in the sharpness of its edges and the frankness of its cuts, and these desirable qualities are promptly obliterated by the use of sandpaper. A sand blast would play havoc with a clever piece of carving, and sandpaper does like harm, only in a lesser degree.

Filing, too, is objectionable. A French writer on wood-carving advises the use of various files to secure a high finish and shows pictures of files of many grades such as are used by sculptors in finishing their marble statues. Now files are quite right to use upon marble, but wood has a different texture, demands a different treatment and calls for cutting tools. The file obliterates that crisp, firm character we seek and enjoy in carved wood. Every craft has its proper tools and we must do the best we can with them and ask no substitutes.

A parallel case is to be found in oil painting, where clever brushwork is the means of expressing form and color. Some artists, dissatisfied with the rough brush marks, introduced the badger blender, a device for smoothing out all inequalities and concealing defects in vague and empty mystery. Fortunately this fashion in painting was of short duration. We admire the bold brushwork of Rembrandt and Sargent, and would not want it lost in higher finish. So, also, we admire bold and rugged carving in wood, provided it is the expression of a purpose to interpret a thing of beauty, not the evidence of a careless or inexperienced hand.

CHAPTER VIII

CARVING IN THE ROUND

WE HAVE thus far considered carving as a decoration having only two dimensions, length and breadth, in spite of the slight relief of its surface. Carving in three dimensions is no different in technique, though presenting some new difficulties. Any rectangular object, presenting four flat surfaces for decoration, like a newel post, may be considered as so many planes, and may be carved accordingly.

But often it becomes necessary to carve a motive detached from a background and visible from all sides. Here the first difficulty encountered lies in the choice of a block of wood of the desired variety, thoroughly seasoned, free from knots, large enough to cut down to the given shape, and having all the fibers parallel to the main axis. The next difficulty is to hold the block rigid while we make our cuts, yet set it free instantly to change its position. The bench vise answers this purpose to a certain extent, but a better contrivance is a carving stand made especially for the purpose. It is like the sculptor's modeling stand, a stool about five feet high, built of heavy timber, having spreading legs for stability, and a firm central column on the upper end of which may be bolted the block of wood for carving. With a support of this sort, the carver may work from all sides, and get new view and new lighting by turning the stand when he wishes.

Where the columnar support of a small table is to be carved, as at D, Fig. 24, I have found it convenient to borrow the family sawbuck, used for sawing logs

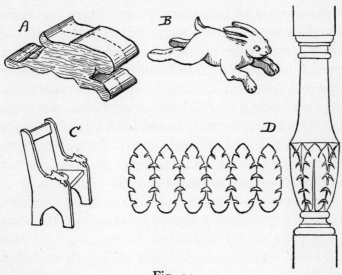

Fig. 24

for the winter fire, and to lay my round object horizontally in it, turning it frequently while carving. This device proved so successful that when I had occasion to decorate two round posts, each ten feet in length, with spirals of foliage, I arranged two saw horses with semicircular notches to hold the posts horizontally, allowing them to turn readily when necessary.

The work of carving consists, as always, in making stop-cuts and slicing out chips, but we soon discover that changes in position often seem to present the grain of the wood in an unexpected direction, and we are suddenly digging in instead of slicing out clean chips. Our only safeguard seems to be in making thin, trial slices before venturing boldly to strike out generous chips with mallet and gouge. Before we begin roughing out our block, we should prepare a model of our motive, in the round and of the exact size to be carved, with all the salient features indicated, omitting minor details. A Michelangelo only could venture to attack a block as he did, without previously determining the ultimate form. We must have a pattern to give us the outline and contour, so that we may measure every part with the calipers as we progress, lest we cut too deep here and there and ruin our work.

For practice in carving in the round let us take a little rabbit such as I carved to ornament the arms of a chair in the Children's Corner in St. John's Church, Washington. A block of oak was chosen whose thickness was exactly that of the body of a rabbit in its widest part. The outline of the animal was traced on the wood and cut out with the band saw, as shown at A in Fig. 24. At half the thickness of the wood a pencil line was drawn all around this cut-out, shown in dotted lines in the figure, to indicate the median plane of the rabbit, as a guide to preserve the bilateral symmetry. A cut one inch wide was made separating the two front paws, and the same was done between the hind paws, then the rabbit was placed astride a sturdy piece of wood one inch thick, and screwed firmly upon it with long screws from below. This piece of wood acted as a firm support to grip in the bench vise while the carving progressed.

The widths of head, shoulders, body, thighs and ears were taken with calipers from a plasticine model already prepared, and the corresponding parts of the block were sliced down to these measurements, spacing one half on each side of the middle line, as nearly as the eye could judge, so that the animal should not get to be "lopsided." Ears and eyes were likewise located and indicated by sharp cuts. The sawed edges of body, head and paws were now rounded off, then the modeling of the skull, the shoulders and the thighs was carefully studied out, emphasizing their anatomy and keeping them in perfect balance with the central plane. Lastly, the forms of the eyes, the orifices of the ears, and indications of the toes were made with sharp, crisp cuts, and the rabbit, removed from its support, was glued in place upon the chair-arm, as seen at C. I should have preferred to carve the rabbit out of the solid wood of the chair but that was impossible in the case, so I was obliged to make it as an applied ornament, in spite of my objections to that practice.

Fig. 25 represents a toy carved by a Russian craftsman, which I have drawn by permission of Mr. H. C. Perleberg, publisher, to show the different stages of production, from the rough block to the finished product. Note that the grain of the wood runs the length of the legs to give them strength to resist breaking.

In Nuremberg I saw the makers of wooden toys employ an ingenious method for blocking out the shapes of wooden animals, as the first stage of carving them for their Noah's Arks. A round disc of wood is sawed from a log of whitewood, across the grain,

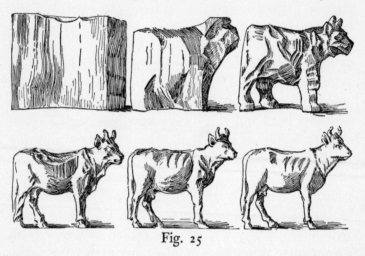

Fig. 25

so that the fibers shall run in the direction of the legs of the toys. The thickness of this disc is a little greater than the height of the animals to be, and it is mounted on the face-plate of a turning lathe, and centered so as to whirl like a wheel. Then it is grooved and shaped to conform to a template till it becomes a ring like a cake known as a "coffee ring," every radial slice of which gives a little animal shape, a camel, an elephant or other, as shown in Fig. 26, accurate in general outline, but requiring the legs to be cut asunder, and the head and body to be deftly modeled. Since, in the finished toy, the entire surface is the product of the carver's tool, this mechanical method of mass production is legitimate from the craftsman's point of view.

In the volume entitled *The Goldsmith of Florence* are pictures of fine statues in wood carved by Mr. Kirchmayer, of Cambridge, Massachusetts, who is probably the foremost wood-carver in this country. His works might well inspire my pupils to attempt

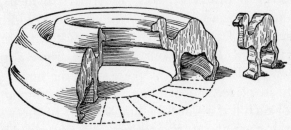

Fig. 26

the highest form of sculpture in wood, but he alone would be capable of instructing them to attain to his lofty degree of perfection. His work is true sculpture, demanding not merely technical skill, but also profound knowledge of the human face and form, besides long years of practical experience in modeling from life.

In France, Dampt and other eminent sculptors sometimes execute busts and statues in wood. One remarkably fine figure is exhibited at the Musée du Luxembourg; but work of this class is beyond the scope of the present volume.

In applying carving to a turned object, the following suggestions may be of value. The turner should be instructed to leave wood sufficient for the thickness of the carving. Fitting a pattern to a round and bulging surface is a practical problem in geometry not to be solved free hand. A case of this occurred in the vase-shaped post of a small Colonial table, or "stand," which I wished to decorate with a sheaf of clustering acanthus leaves, as seen in Fig. 24-D. I measured the circumference of the post in its thickest part by means of a strip of drawing paper, and this I divided into six equal parts, each part representing the width of one acanthus leaf. I drew the leaf, repeated six times, edge to edge, and cut out the whole paper pattern and wrapped it around the post, tying the upper part snugly in place, and bending down and pinning the base of each leaf against the bulbous part of the wood. Then I marked the six outlines on the wood, and carved the leaves as if each were on a flat surface, turning the post so as to bring one leaf uppermost, after another was finished.

Two laundry posts which I undertook to carve presented a new problem in laying out a pattern on a cylindrical surface, as they were to be decorated with two spiral bands of ferns and fronds, separated by plain spiral spaces.

I cut two long strips of paper in width equal to the decorative bands, and wrapped these around the posts in a spiral, taking great care that the spaces between should be everywhere the same. I tied them at short intervals and traced their edges in spiral lines on the wood. The repeating pattern of ferns and fronds being cut out of stencil paper, I applied it to fit the appointed space between the lines, and repeatedly outlined it till the band was filled from base to summit. In carving, I first cut away the plain spiral space to the depth of ¼ of an inch, and rounded and smoothed the wood with great care, so that it should represent the post clasped by the ferns and fronds.

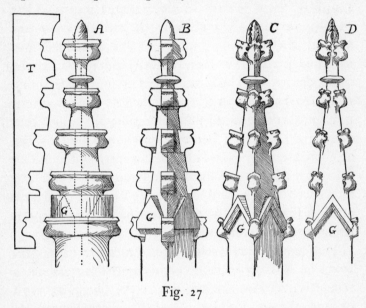

Fig. 27

New difficulties developed when I undertook to carve Gothic pinnacles ornamented with crockets, for in trying to work free-hand, these crockets refused to line up either vertically or horizontally, since I was constantly cutting away my guiding lines. Then I resorted to the following scheme, illustrated in Fig. 27. C is the outline presented by the pinnacle, showing the widest view of it, seen from one angle. I cut a template, T, to fit this outline, and to include the gables. On the turning lathe I then turned a block shown at A, to match the template, with a series of rings, each ring enclosing four crockets. Dividing the lower circumference into four equal parts, I drew from base to apex four guide lines, dotted in A, to represent the edges of the little roof and the middle of each crocket. Then I marked half the width of each crocket on either side of its guide line, and also sketched the location of each little gable on the cylindrical part, G. With these lines established, I found it a simple matter to slice out the flat surface of the pyramidal roof, and to cut out flat sides of the crockets, as seen in B. These latter were rounded into shape as shown on the left of C, and carved into Gothic foliations as seen on the right. Each little gable was first sliced to the dotted lines, then carved as shown at G in C and D. D gives a view of the finished pinnacle seen from one side.

In general, when carving in the round, whether the work be symmetrical or not, it is always possible to trace one view of the subject on the block, and saw this out, then replacing the cut-off pieces whence they came and holding them in position with strings or brads, to turn the block on its side, trace upon it another view and cut it out as before. In this way a great mass of useless wood will be disposed of quickly, leaving the subject approximately blocked out in three dimensions. Then templates and calipers may be used with good effect to arrive rapidly at the exact dimensions.

CHAPTER IX

CARVING IN THE GOTHIC MANNER

IN ORDER to enjoy his hobby the wood-carver does not actually require to know the history and development of his craft. Yet a knowledge of these matters will add to his appreciation of fine old wood-carving, and give unity to his own productions.

The architecture of a building determines the style of its furniture and woodwork, and the carved embellishments of the latter must be in harmony with the whole.

In building the great churches and cathedrals of the Middle Ages a special style of architecture was developed which we think of as peculiarly ecclesiastical, and this style was copied in the interior woodwork and furniture, the sculpture in stone serving as models for the wood-carvers to follow in their decorative details.

This ecclesiastical style is called Gothic, but quite incorrectly so, since the Goths flourished and faded out of history centuries before the great cathedrals came into being. The common usage of the term compels us, however, to apply the name of the barbarian Goths to the works of expert engineers and builders of the twelfth and thirteenth centuries, who were truly modernists of their epoch. It is not generally known that the system invented to make possible the construction of "Gothic" cathedrals is in principle very like our modern steel skyscraper construction, and was as great an innovation. The features which had influence on wood-carving were the rose windows and those with pointed arches, all divided into patterns by intricate tracery. Besides these, the mouldings, leaf forms and quaint faces and figures which appear in stone sculpture, all are found repeated in wood adorning the interiors of churches and monasteries.

The pointed arches had no fixed and established proportion of breadth compared with height, but were

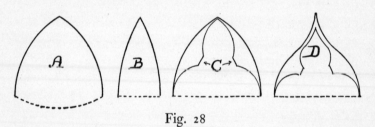

Fig. 28

rarely wider than the radius of their curve (see Fig. 28-A). Pointed arches frequently occur as the basis of the pattern on a carved panel, and in designing such a panel we can venture to strike the arcs with a radius as great as the width to be decorated, as in A; or greater, if a very acute arch, as at B, is desired. Gothic arches often bear "cusps," or prominences projecting inward, as at C, and these give marked character to a Gothic arch. Arches were sometimes given an ogee curve, as at D, producing an especially acute apex. A series of arches, side by side, and without tracery, produces a simple surface decoration, applicable to a pulpit, a reredos or a wainscoting. When the space is extensive the flat surface within each arch calls for much monotonous toil in carving out and smoothing up in proper manner, and in this case it seems quite permissible for the carver to cut out his arches and apply them to flat, smooth panels. Small panels to form part of a piece of furniture should never be treated in this manner, but should be carved out of solid wood.

In the Gothic period glass was manufactured only in small pieces, and these, united into leaded panes of moderate size, required the support of mullions or ornamental tracery to fill the huge cathedral windows, hence we derive the window patterns so intricate and alluring, made more varied by repetition of cusps on nearly every curve.

Tracery of windows was promptly copied by the wood-carver in all its lacelike complexities. He plainly took delight in making new and ingenious combinations for his patterns, and we, too, can display our own originality in laying out tracery for our carving. A few Gothic panels are outlined in Fig. 29, copied from old, carved chests, to show what pleasing variety may be derived from the use of arches and tracery.

In laying out a pattern of this sort, when the arch and its major divisions are accurately drawn, it is better to depend upon the eye in establishing the curves of the small details, rather than upon the rigid curves struck by the compass, for in that way our lines will flow more suavely and our openings will have more grace. When one-half of the pattern seems satisfactory, it may be turned over upon the opposite side and repeated on the other half of the panel by means of tracing paper, so as to preserve the symmetry of the composition. Examination of old Gothic panels reveals that the designer worked free-hand and was uncramped by mechanical limitations, for his curves are rarely arcs of circles, and his pattern is not a slavish repetition of units. Good wood-carving is neither rigidly mechanical, nor carelessly sloven, nor yet capriciously irregular, but is the outcome of a skilled

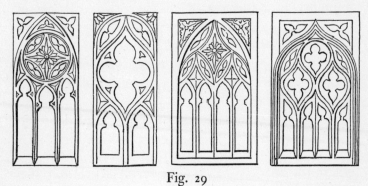

Fig. 29

hand and a trained eye, impressing the work with human interest.

In examining Gothic patterns we discover a certain decorative unit recurring many times, characteristic of the period. This is the shape A, Fig. 30, made by the intersection of two arcs of circles, suggesting a fish, a symbol chosen in early days to represent the Christian religion, for which reason it was appropriate to repeat this motive throughout the carved ornamentation of ecclesiastical architecture and furniture. As this motive more nearly resembles the shape of a lifeboat, or

the Venetian gondola, pointed at bow and stern, I prefer to designate it as the "boat motive." These boats
were generally cusped, as shown in B, Fig. 31, in plan
and section. It is well to practice this oft-repeated motive so as to carve it with facility, proceeding in the following manner: Trace the shape of the boat, and make
a deep stop-cut from bow to stern as shown at A;
scoop out the hull with a gouge fitting the curvature,
and paying attention to the direction of your cuts in
reference to the grain of the wood; in the center,

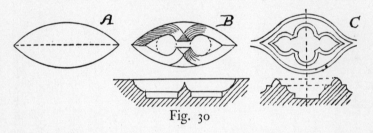

Fig. 30

where the work is to go to a deeper level, sketch in
the two balloon-shaped outlines, and sink the openings as shown in the section B, and cut away the wood
between the cusps. Sometimes our boat motive is
curved to fill a given space, as in two of the panel
designs given in Fig. 29, but the only change in carving would be to curve the first deep stop-cut.

Sometimes in carving the boat motive it is found
convenient to bore out the deepest part adjoining the
cusps with a flat-nosed bit, called a Forstner bit, which
exactly fits the pattern at this point, as shown in dotted
lines in B, quickly removing the surplus wood, and
slicing down into these holes to make the shape of

the hull, after which the deep points may be sunk with chisel and spoon chisel. A shape similar to the boat was often employed, shown at C, having ogee curves for outline, and two cusps. This motive may be carved precisely like the boat, sinking each level, and sketching the deeper design, then proceeding as before.

An enrichment added to the double cusped pattern consists in a pearl and flower-shape suggestive of our native dogwood blossom shown in Fig. 31, and in sec-

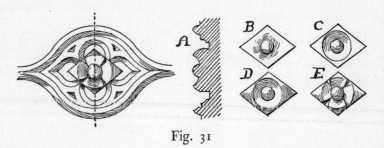

Fig. 31

tion at A. The carving of the central feature is shown in four progressive stages at B, C, D and E.

A diamond or lozenge shape may be decorated with cusps and central ornament, making a fine decoration to repeat over a surface. Where thus employed in antique wood-carving, we find monotonous repetition relieved occasionally by filling one row of diamonds with fleurs-de-lis, but as this flower was the symbol of royalty in France, we too often see that this graceful flower design has been rudely hacked off by iconoclastic "citizens" during the Revolution.

Pierced carving is frequently found in Gothic work, giving an airy, lacelike effect. Any of the patterns in

Fig. 29 may be so treated, and in Fig. 32 are three designs copied from an old French church, which may be found useful.

The designing of the tracery to fill a great rose window gave scope for play of fancy to the architect, and the wood-carver found equal delight in filling circular patterns with intricate carved filigree. We may enjoy much the same sport, evolving new combinations to fill circular spaces. The simplest filling of the circle is with trefoil, quatrefoil, etc., formed

Fig. 32

by three, four or more cusps within the circle. More complex and alluring combinations may be made with the fish motive and curved triangles and polygons. Here we are free to exercise our ingenuity, and get all the fun out of making new and intricate combinations.

A simple panel decoration extensively used by Gothic wood-carvers was the "linen fold" or "parchment fold" already referred to, and illustrated in Fig. 18, more examples of which are given in Fig. 33. The surface presents a series of rolls and curved channels, as indicated by the sections below each sketch, supposed to represent rolls and folds of linen or parchment. To produce this undulating surface, we first rabbet the sides of our panel, then cut the grooves with a combination plane, and mould the edges of the projections in like manner, till the desired profile is obtained. Then we rabbet the ends of the panel, lay out the design to suggest the rolled or folded material,

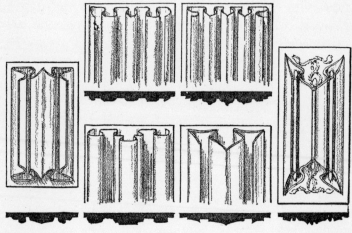

Fig. 33

and carve the same as we see in the designs given. Where several panels are to have the same sectional profile, we may save labor by cutting a long board to the width, then channeling and moulding the board all its length, cutting it up into panels, and proceeding as above. Some carvers became so ambitious to produce realistic effects in wood that they represented their parchments with sticks to roll them upon. The panel on the right of Fig. 33 shows a panel carved in this manner, drawn at the Musée des Arts Decoratifs.

But embellishments purely architectural and geometrical could not long satisfy the carvers in stone and wood, whose opulent fancy soon burst into an exuberant growth of foliage and of flowers. The pagan acanthus leaf they had apparently forgotten, or at least they preferred to replace it as a decorative element by the native flora. When we examine the ornamental carving of an old church in France, we are almost sure to discover that the carver has derived his motives of leaves, flowers and seed vessels from the nearby countryside, and, conventionalizing them to meet his requirements, has carved them with loving care and skill.

Violett-le-Duc, who was the most painstaking student of the Gothic churches, mentions the following plants he has identified in this botany of decoration: flowers of the arum, iris, perennial pea, snapdragon, orchid, leaves of oak, pear, plantain, primrose, columbine, grape, watercress and thistle; fruits of grape, fig and strawberry.

Let us take the hint from these examples, and make use of motives chosen from our own native wildflowers, conventionalizing them, subjecting them to the laws of decoration, and evolving new and beautiful patterns for our wood-carving.

A good decoration was generally built upon some geometrical plan, which we will explain by the following example:

It is desired to plan a pattern consisting of a grapevine bearing fruit, leaves and tendrils. The leaves, the most important element, are drawn to fit a square shape, as we see in Fig. 34, and this square is repeated, as in the dotted diagram below, at equal intervals and staggered alternately. The vine is now trained as a scroll first above then below these alternating squares. The bunches of grapes are next sketched in the intervals between the leaves, and connected to the vine

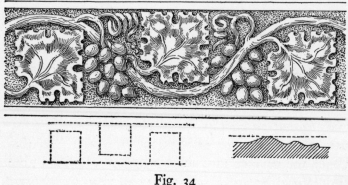

Fig. 34

in a convincing manner, and any vacant spaces are filled with tendrils. To assist the carver, a section of a leaf along the midrib is given to show how the undulations of the surface should rise and fall.

Botanical motives were not commonly used to decorate panels and flat surfaces, but were extensively applied to columns, crockets and finials, and enlivened the crown-ornaments above the rood screens and canopies.

In addition to the luxuriant foliage, the medieval carvers produced a vast zoölogy of strange animals, of beasts inspired by the Apocalypse, animals occurring in the realm of heraldry, monsters out of legendary lore, birds and fishes bred in travelers' minds. No need was here of truth and realism, but convincing power of narration. Quaint human heads occur in profusion carved on cornices and beam-ends, some of them with humorous, others with pained expressions. Human figures, lacking both proportion and anatomy, give us lively pictures of contemporary life and ruling emotions. In the choir stalls the seats were made to lift, and in the under sides of them were attached little shelves or brackets, planned to give a certain amount of support to standing singers during the long and monotonous chanting. These were called "Misericordes," and were carved with figure compositions in endless variety, many of them quite Rabelaisian in subject, but abounding in quaint conceits. When the devotee to wood-carving takes a trip to the Old World he will find keen enjoyment in forming the acquaintance of this hidden population of the churches, in England and France, and return home inspired, perhaps, to adapt scenes of American life to a similar treatment in wood-carving.

Chapter X

RENAISSANCE CARVING

Wood-carving of the Gothic style had been developed by brethren of monastic orders, then taught and practiced by guilds of carvers composed of apprentices, journeymen and master carvers. The rules of the guilds and the canons of the craft had become firmly established, and wood-carving had made itself one of the arts of the Middle Ages.

Then, because certain scholars in Italy took to studying the culture of antiquity, and architects and sculptors became enamoured of the beauty of Greek temples and Roman statues, all medieval work became discredited, viewed as the work of Goths and barbarians, and our wood-carvers were forced to change their principles or starve.

The revival of interest in classical literature led to a study of antique decorative arts, and in consequence the wood-carver was obliged to learn a whole series of new motives to ornament the furniture and woodwork newly come into fashion.

This art of the Renaissance, beginning in Italy about 1450, swept across Western Europe and migrated to America with the early colonists, leaving its impress upon architecture, decoration and furniture, and the resulting transformations are exceedingly interesting to

follow—but as a wood-carver, I must confine myself to
noting the new motives which came with this intel-
lectual revolution, referring to the furniture only as
it interests the wood-carver, either helping him to

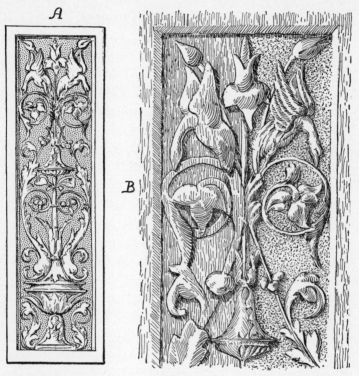

Fig. 35

recognize the epoch of antique wood-carving, or to
make his own productions harmonious and free from
anachronisms.

The first new motive the carver had to learn was
the Renaissance panel decoration, copied from Roman

pilasters. From the bottom of the panel, or from an elegant vase, there sprouts a strange plant or tree, whose single erect stem divides the panel into two equal parts, and branches symmetrically into graceful spirals of foliage. This plant becomes a sort of Christmas tree looped with ribbons and strings of pearls, upon whose branches the carver hangs all manner of objects, musical instruments, trophies of fishing and the chase, products of the land and sea, and entwines the tendrils about cherubs, strange birds and dolphins, all placed in perfectly balanced symmetry, and rendered with ineffable grace and charm. A pattern of this style is given in Fig. 35 at A, for the student to copy, and at B a portion of the same on a scale twice as large, showing on the left side the ground sunken to ⅜ of an inch, and the chief features roughly blocked in.

The slender vines and tendrils should not be carved down from the surface, but where they occur the wood should be sunken about ⅜ of an inch, the vine sketched and outlined with the veining tool on either side, then the ground around it may be cut down to the full depth of ⅜ of an inch leaving the vine ¼ inch in projection, to be rounded off with less danger of crumbling away in the process.

The right side of B shows further progress in the work of carving; the background is smoothed and stippled; the leaves are carefully modeled, and their curving movement rendered by bold and sweeping strokes of the tool; the feathers of the birds are frankly indicated without attempts at copying real texure.

Narrow, upright panels like this, copied from one in the Cluny Museum, Paris, became popular throughout Europe, and were used in wainscots, newel posts, the closed portions of wooden screens, and the fronts of thousands of beautiful chests.

Sometimes a long, low panel was to be carved for an overdoor, a mantel, or a chest whose front was made of a single plank or panel. Here again the space is divided by a vertical axis of symmetry with the cartouche as a central motive, which was invented in this period, and which has been described in Chapter IV. This is flanked on either hand by human figures or mythical animals whose bodies merge into the stems of exquisite scrolls adorned with leaves and flowers.

Half a panel is shown in Fig. 36-A where the important feature to be noted is the way in which the leaves grow. Here and there upon the stem appears a little knot or cluster, C, resembling the calyx of a flower called a "culot" and out of this springs the leaf, which follows and clasps the stem. The stem, twisting into a spiral, often terminates in a flower, the center of which protrudes into a sort of trumpet filled with pearls. It is supposed that these pearls, bursting forth and scattering, are intended to represent pollen, or possibly ripened seeds.

The accompanying Fig. 36-B should be carved as a study for the treatment of the clasping leaf. First notice that the leaf stands boldly away from the ground on the lower edge, to give strong shadow, but slopes gently backward on the upper side till it nearly dies off into the background along the upper points.

Disregarding points and indentations, as indicated by dotted lines, the leaf should be roughed out to give this bold edge and backward slope. Then, sketching in the most important indentations, make a straight cut with the carving knife, between serrations, and work

A

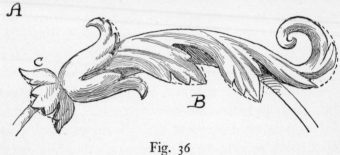

C

B

Fig. 36

from the points on either side, into this stop-cut, thus you will avoid breaking the wood at its weakest point.

The modeling must be executed with bold sweeps of the tool, leaving some of the veins in sharp relief.

The "culot" is blocked out as a lump with three lobes, then it is refined in the usual manner. There should be no undercutting of leaves or stems.

The exuberant fancy of the Renaissance artists soon broke away from the fixed canons of classical architecture, and in playful mood designed Ionic and Corinthian capitals enlivened with masks and dolphins, festoons and garlands. They gave their columns fantastic outlines, and encrusted them with ornaments. They even played pranks with the staid outline of the pediment of the classic temple, breaking out a portion of the pointed gable, often curving the broken mouldings and enriching them with rosettes and garlands.

A door-cap made up of straight mouldings is a work belonging strictly to the cabinetmaker or joiner, but that with curved mouldings calls for the skill of the wood-carver. A stout, flat board should form the backing of the entire door-cap, against which the different sections are fastened with screws. The two curved mouldings and the garland with rosettes must be sawed out separately, carved and adjusted to fill their spaces, then fastened in place and retouched with carving tools wherever necessary. In case this pediment is to crown an exterior doorway, a coat of oil paint, preferably of white lead, should be given to all the layers and joints when fixing them upon the backboard.

The broken pediment remained a favorite motive for designers of furniture down to our own day, and was especially popular in our "black walnut period," in President Grant's administration, when our best and noblest trees were slaughtered to make our worst furniture.

The cartouche, described in Chapter IV, was derived from the shield or buckler of a knight, with his coat of arms emblazoned upon it, the rolled and twisted edges representing the leather composing the shield. In place of an escutcheon the center of the cartouche was later filled by an elliptical or oval shape, and domed, as shown in Fig. 36. This decorative feature was named a "cabochon," and was very often carved as a separate piece and glued on.

These motives, and many others invented by the Italian designers, were copied in every land where the impulse of the Renaissance movement was felt. And though in Italy after 1600 the initial force was lost in excessive ornament, yet in France, England, Spain and the Netherlands the Renaissance exercised a vital influence for two centuries longer.

When the French kings, Charles VIII and Francis I, invaded Italy, they intended only to capture and annex certain provinces, but when they beheld the beautiful works of Renaissance art, then in its prime, they determined to capture and bring back to their own land this vivid Renaissance spirit. So they acquired numberless fine works of art, and induced a small army of artists, craftsmen and artificers to return with them to teach the principles of their work in France. The seed thus imported grew into a flourishing plant and became naturalized in the royal domain, where it transformed grim castles into fairy palaces, and imparted to the woodwork a grace and elegance before unknown. In the Loire district are splendid specimens of carved furniture, mantels and wainscots.

The strap carving, described in Chapter III, was extensively used, especially to adorn the panels of stately portals.

The increasing luxury of the court and the nobility gave plenty of work to the wood-carvers, but no distinctive direction to the design till the time of Louis XIV, when each room of the vast palaces became a problem, with furniture, walls, cornices and

Fig. 37

doors all designed and executed as a unit of harmonious decorative art.

The excellence of the carving of the stately furniture is too often concealed by excessive gilding; but the wall-panels present elegant examples of the art, and, fortunately for us, some fine examples of this and succeeding periods may be seen and studied in the Morgan Collection at the Metropolitan Museum in New York. The two characteristic motives of the style of Louis XIV are the initial letters L. L. interlaced under a royal crown, and the face of the blazing sun, symbol of "le Roi Soleil." See Fig. 37. The shell motive is but one of the vast number which went to embellish the work of the period. In examining original work, the student should notice that the boards making up these splendid panels were grooved-and-tongued and glued together, and designs were carried across the seams. Also, carving of the best period is invariably sliced out of solid wood, never applied. The labor of sinking and smoothing the ground is enormous, but some of this toil is avoided by the device of leaving the ground untouched in the middle of the panel, and sinking it only at the upper and lower ends, where ornamental devices are to be given relief as seen in Fig. 37. A panel so treated is called a "fielded panel."

Under Louis XV came a distinct departure from the strict formalism of previous designs. Every line was given a curve, and every form a distorted outline. Strict symmetry in composition was discarded, yet a certain precarious balance of the parts was maintained, producing charming and unexpected effects. A new element, characteristic of the period, was the motive called "rocaille," an ornate edge suggestive of the fluted lip of a shell, or the rippling border of a wave, shown in the drawing of a panel in Fig. 38. This frequently gives character to a complicated mass of vines and leaves.

The wood-carvers in Louis XV's time must have been busy men, for all the curves of panels, armchairs, picture frames, bedsteads must have been shaped by carving tools, and in most cases ornamented with exquisite leaf forms and arabesques. Then the warped

and bulged surfaces of furniture required carving and
shaping up before they received their finish of veneer,
inlaying or decorative painting. These forms were
always elegant, never grotesque.

If the wood-carver is attracted by the shapes of
Louis XV design, he can have real fun with his hobby
in making small objects in that spirit, such as jewel

Fig. 38

caskets, trays, boxes for cards, cigarettes and other
uses. None but a carver can produce these things, for
the surfaces are all curved, rounded and hollowed in
a way to preclude machine work.

I have watched with keen delight young Italian
craftsmen, men who seemed most ordinary workmen,
turn out these dainty little art objects with ease and
precision, coat them with gesso, paint them with float-
ing ribbons and garlands of flowers, and then "antique" them with a brownish varnish. Only the date
of 1750 was needed to make them true to their epoch.

These lads had one good model to copy, giving them all the waves and bulges of the surface, and a slight suggestion of "rocaille ornament."

On the accession of Louis XVI and Marie Antoinette came a return to nature and the simple life. And this change of purpose immediately impressed itself upon the art and the furniture of the new reign. A con-

Fig. 39

tributing factor was the discovery of a new source of inspiration, a new assortment of motives in the excavations of the buried cities of Pompeii and Herculaneum. Up to that time, classical inspiration had come from study of grandiose ruins of temples and palaces, but the new discoveries brought to light classical objects for the intimate use of the home. Their value was appreciated as models for productions in the period. In 1749 the architect Soufflot, the artist Cochin, and the Marquis de Vandière went officially to study these discoveries, and in Italy joined company with Robert Adam, who was to introduce the new spirit into England.

In France, straight lines and balanced compositions were restored, slender columns and finely carved mouldings became the fashion, the bow-knot and the garland were considered ample embellishment. Fig. 39 shows a chair-leg, a mirror frame and a bracket, with the restrained carving of the period.

In America we have become familiar with the style of this period because of its influence on our own so-called Colonial, but the slender construction and low relief gave little opportunity for the wood-carver to exercise his skill.

After the French Revolution, the wood-carver became quite subservient to the cabinetmaker, and contributed nothing to the originality of design.

In Flanders the impulse of the Renaissance had been at work moulding a national style, two motives of which were extensively borrowed and copied in other lands, namely, the "Flemish scroll" and the spiral column.

The former is a scroll, appearing in two forms, the letter C and the letter S. It appears in chair-backs, and in stretchers between chair-legs, also in the crowning members of cupboards and bookcases. See Fig. 40-A and B. Boldly carved, occasionally pierced, it held popularity through the years till it became lost in the confusion of meaningless twists we see in Victorian furniture.

The spiral column was extensively used in the Neth-

erlands and later in England for table-legs, sides of
chair-backs, stair spindles. Today these are turned out
by machinery, and if our wood-carver is intent upon
introducing them in his work, he can, of course, order
them made for him, but it is evident that in the seventeenth century they were made by hand, and it seems

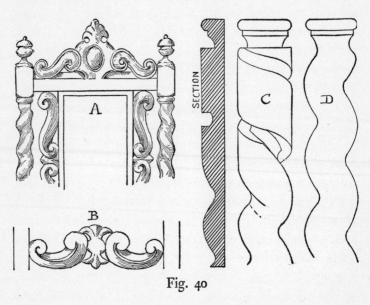

Fig. 40

that the true wood-carver should take such pride in his
work as to wish to execute these difficult pieces with
his own hand.

In order to do this, it is first necessary to make an
accurate drawing, full size, of the twisted column, as
it is to appear when finished, and to cut a template of
stiff tin to fit accurately the profile, D, Fig. 40.

Select a piece of wood free of knots, and having

the grain running as nearly as possible parallel to the length, turn this in the lathe to a cylinder having a diameter exactly that of the outside of the column; at the same time form the moulding on the base and capital, in accordance with the drawing. Next, lay out on the cylinder a spiral to represent the inner and thinner part of our column. From the drawing we see that the spiral advances a certain amount at every turn, called the "pitch," in this case exactly two inches, so, drawing a straight line on the cylinder, parallel to the axis, lay off 2″, 4″, 6″, etc., to indicate 1, 2 and 3 turns of the spiral. Then wrap a narrow strip of stiff paper around the cylinder, making a spiral from the base through the 2″, 4″ and 6″ points, and so on to the end, and trace this spiral line upon the wood. This line represents the innermost portion of our spiral column, and we must excavate a trench following this spiral line. Laying the column horizontally, make a great many saw-cuts for a stop-cut along our spiral line, at short intervals, taking care never to cut too deep, then with chisel and mallet cut out a spiral V-shaped groove the whole length of the cylinder, as shown in C and the bottom of this round with a gouge. The upper edges of the groove should also be rounded off, as at D, so as to approach the profile of the column. When the cylinder is thus "roughed out," take the template and work one side of the wood to fit it from end to end, then giving the wood ⅛ of a turn, or about 45 degrees, cut another profile to approximate the template which is slipped up a distance equal to ⅛ of the "pitch."

Thus, by frequent turns and advances of the template to keep pace with the spiral groove, cut eight or more profiles so nearly adjacent that they serve for guides to the final modeling of the column. This is accomplished by delicate slices with chisels and gouges, depending upon the eye, but making frequent tests with the template, and also trying with the calipers the thickness of the spiral, a measurement made,

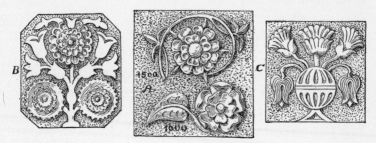

Fig. 41

not perpendicular to the axis, as in ordinary lathe-turning, but perpendicular to the spiral.

In the Yale Art School are some fine ancient confessionals ornamented with twisted columns, all carved by hand, their inner spirals filled with garlands of flowers and vines, which greatly add to their beauty, but must have involved immense labor in the execution.

The artistic impulse of the Renaissance reached England considerably later than France, but was introduced in very much the same manner, for, like the French kings, Henry VIII came under its spell and sent for Italian artists, craftsmen and artificers, to de-

sign and embellish his palace of Nonesuch, and make
it a place of surpassing splendor. The Renaissance
carving was called "Romayne work" and "Anticke
work," and the date of its coming is established by
the choir stalls in this style, in Kings College, Cambridge, given by Henry, and marked with his initials,
and those of Anne Boleyn, placing the date about

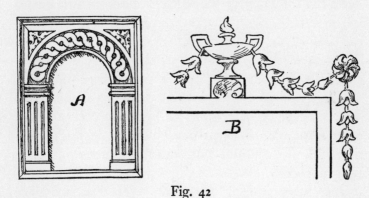

Fig. 42

1530-1535. Under Elizabeth carving followed Italian
models, but with the impress of English taste. A motive introduced at this time was the so-called "Tudor
rose" shown in the Fig. 41-A, which will be found
a useful subject to introduce in patterns of this period.

The Jacobean period, justly called the "Golden
Age of Oak" has bequeathed to us a glorious heritage
of furniture and woodwork, solid, robust, richly
carved with original designs, first of which we must
mention the round arch. Chests, chair-backs and bedsteads received this motive, shown in Fig. 42-A. It is
a souvenir of the classical arch supported on fluted

pilasters, with a suggestion of capital and base. The
archivolt is often carved with the guilloche and the
spandrils filled with three leaves surrounding a pearl.
The space within the arch was sometimes left plain,
but more often enriched with a floral pattern. Fig.
41, B and C show two flower forms, one the sun-
flower, and another favorite the tulip, which we dis-
cussed in Chapter III. The latter recalls an interesting
bit of history, since it originated in Holland at about
the time of the "tulip craze."

Chairs with high backs, paneled and carved, are
called "wainscot chairs." High backs were only for
the "seats of the mighty"—kings, bishops and nobles.
The humble were content to sit upon stools. This
caste distinction is perpetuated with us in the chair-
man of a meeting, one supposed to have the exclusive
right to a chair.

The parts of oak furniture were mortised and
pinned together with dowel pins, never glued, and the
mouldings around panels were worked on the edges
of stiles and rails, not applied as separate pieces,
mitered in the corners.

A piece of oak furniture which has now gone out
of fashion was the Bible box. The family Bible was
cherished with great care, and lodged in a box ex-
pressly made and handsomely carved. And, unlike
other boxes and chests, it had no lock, because a
thief would not steal a Bible. One or more of these
boxes are in the Metropolitan Museum, which, with
their excellent design in shallow carving, will be useful
models for the carver to copy.

Walnut wood became a favorite in the reign of Charles II inducing the wood-carver to produce work of a higher finish, but inlaying, veneer and lacquer crowded out some of the carved embellishments.

We should here note a motive which was introduced about this time, since it first appears carved upon a chair dated 1686. This was the garland composed of flowers called "Garrya elliptica," see Fig. 42-B, which were strung together and beautifully graduated as to size like pearls in a well-graded necklace. Festoons of it were draped around vases, over mirrors, and enlivened many inlayed patterns. Each blossom is carved like the "culot" and is connected with its neighbor by a cord. When carved, they should be given ample support by thick wood at the back.

The introduction of mahogany in 1720 naturally brought about considerable change in wood-carving. It replaced the bold and robust technique peculiar to oak-carving with delicate outline and subtle modeling. Chippendale, appreciating the beauty and excellence of mahogany, designed and carved his furniture in this wood with masterly skill. His most characteristic motive was a bow of fluttering ribbon intwined in the backs of his chairs.

Many other motives were used, such as finely carved acanthus leaves clasping the uprights and arms of chairs, and rocaille ornaments upon the curves of cabriole legs, rendered in such low relief as to be almost invisible.

From now onward, through the times of Hepplewhite, Sheraton and Adam, carving was graceful in design and exquisite in execution. But it occupied a place subordinate to the work of the cabinetmaker, and need occupy our attention no further.

In America we can trace a distinct inclination for wood-carving in the early Colonial days, as shown in the Hadley and Connecticut chests. Furniture imported from England, France and the Netherlands gave us examples to follow, and books of design published abroad were eagerly sought and followed by our craftsmen, so that good work was done in line with foreign traditions.

Boston, Deerfield, the Hudson River Valley, Philadelphia and Virginia all possess fine specimens of carving, Salem furnishing especially interesting examples in work by Samuel Macentyre, a master designer and carver, a genius in a carpenter's apron.

A well-preserved and complete example of early American wood-carving is to be seen at Gunniston Hall in Virginia. The walls of each room, from floor to ceiling, are covered with panels beautifully designed and carved. I understand that the Hall may be visited (through proper introduction), and the wood-carver will find keen delight in studying these interiors.

The following information will interest him also, taken from the *Gentleman's Magazine* of 1781 and quoted by Mr. Charles O. Cornelius in his *Early American Furniture*:

"The American stoves are much superior to any before invented. These stoves are called American, because the first patterns of them, in cast iron, were the invention of Dr. Benjamin Franklin." They were cast in the Adam designs of the period, and, as we all know, patterns for casting are made in wood, and carved wherever ornament is required in the casting. What interesting relics we should consider these casting patterns, showing design of Adam, under the influence of Pompeiian discoveries—if only we were able to find them.

CHAPTER XI

CARVED MOULDINGS

MOULDINGS are studied and represented by the curved line or "profile" they present when taken in section. It might seem that mouldings are such minor members of a design that they could be disregarded, but archæologists have shown that certain mouldings go with certain epochs, changing with changing styles, and that they furnish an index of the culture and refinement of the builders and craftsmen.

Greek mouldings were generally drawn free-hand, with subtle appreciation of the effect of light and shadow they would produce. Roman builders, less sensitive to artistic values, usually struck the profiles of their mouldings with the compass, and the models they established were followed during and after the Renaissance period. Gothic mouldings, however, bore small resemblance to those of classical times, were usually drawn free-hand, with curves other than arcs of circles, and had a great variety of contours.

The amateur designer and carver will naturally desire to have his mouldings correspond in period with other features of his design, and for this he has the advantage over the commercial manufacturer in that he can afford to expend the necessary time and effort in research and in labor in order to make his design correct in all its parts.

Gothic Mouldings. The Gothic chest seems to have been the most important piece of furniture of the period, if we may judge by the great number preserved in museums and private collections in Europe. Those I have examined never were furnished with mouldings under the edges of the lids, nor applied mouldings surrounding the panels. If any moulding appears, it is worked with a moulding plane on the

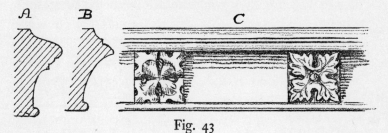

Fig. 43

vertical stiles till they meet the rails, and upon the upper rail only along the top of each panel. The top and side mouldings are made to join one another by carving out portions of the upper rail. The lower rail of the chest is chamfered off at an angle of 45 degrees, and the lower ends of the vertical mouldings are made to die off upon this slope. Often a V groove is run outside the mouldings, and around the upper corners in quarter-circles.

On other furniture, like the "credence," and the "dressoir," the overhanging top had a moulded edge, and was supported by a moulding underneath. One type of this sort is shown in profile at A in Fig. 43.

At B is the profile of a moulding often seen crowning the panels of wainscoting. As seen in front view at C, it is frequently ornamented with rosettes. The carver, true to his craft, might feel it necessary to work out by hand the hollow profile in the intervals between the rosettes, making constant tests with a template to assist him in keeping the proper curve, but he should be allowed to run the moulding with a moulding plane, from end to end, and to carve his rosettes separately, setting them in place neatly and at regular intervals. Where this moulding is placed above paneling the

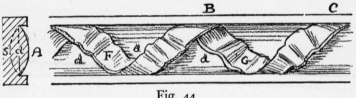

Fig. 44

rosettes should be arranged to center over the vertical stiles. Any other spacing or arrangement will look "queer."

Where a ribbon is carved, as in Fig. 44, copied from woodwork in the Cathedral of Amiens, a convex profile should first be made, as at A, upon which the front spirals of the ribbon are sketched, as at B C, then the diamond-shaped interval between B and C is sunk down to the dotted line, d, in the section, and on this level the lower return spirals F G are sketched, and the triangular spaces, d d, are sliced out down to a lower level, forming a concave profile, as at S, so that the ribbon will seem to lie in a half-round trough.

The ribbon can then be given a great variety of sprightly waves and undulations to suit the fancy of the carver.

Where a moulding is sufficiently wide to accommodate a leaf pattern, sometimes we find a running vine used as embellishment. Upon the curved moulding leaves are sketched. The spaces between are then sunk to the level of the sinuous stem, and this is now sketched in. Lastly, the background is sunk to form a coved profile giving deep shadows for relief of the

Fig. 45

vine. In Chapter X we have shown how a leaf-and-vine may be laid out, on a system of squares, and this method is perfectly applicable to a moulding.

A moulding pattern found in Gothic churches in England, shown in Fig. 45, will be found useful. It presents agreeable variety of parts, a flowing line, a suggestion of leafage, and bright, round accents like fruit. Begin with a quarter-round moulding, seen in profile at O, measure the chord of the quarter-round arc and double this to get the length of one repeat, M N. Sketch in the little round "fruits" and draw the vine sweeping down and up in a sinuous line. Fit in the leaf forms, and connect some of them with the fruits. The space between M and N thus will form the repeating pattern, to be copied the whole length of the moulding.

In carving this motive one should preserve as far as possible the original convex surface O, but the stem must wave and twist with suave undulations, and the fruits must stand out crisp and round to give sharp contrasts of light and shade. This motive works well on a small scale, as in the Gothic credence shown in Fig. 18, and I have also used it on a large scale to ornament the barge-boards on the exterior gable of a

Fig. 46

half-timber residence, where sun and shadow play agreeably upon the design.

A carved moulding frequently used for both horizontal and vertical members, was called the leaf-and-stick pattern shown in Fig. 46; the section may be a half-round, or may have a somewhat flatter profile. Sketch out the outer leaves B B at equal intervals, cut down their spiral outlines to the first level, leaving the "stick" in relief, as at S in section, and having stubs of branches showing at intervals, T T. Lastly round the stick, cut veins in the leaves and notch their edges with a small gouge.

Carved mouldings were more common in England

than on the Continent. In France, especially, the
Gothic designer lavished his carving on flat surfaces,
reserving his mouldings to produce strong lines of
shadow to accent the construction.

Renaissance Mouldings. The architects and designers of the Renaissance revived the mouldings of Classic
Rome most of which were struck with the compass.

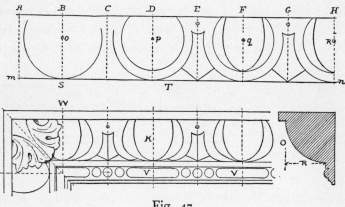

Fig. 47

We shall treat only those which are especially adapted
for carving, such as the ovolo, or quarter-round,
shown in Fig. 47 in section at O, in front view at K,
and developed in T.

We will proceed to design the familiar egg-and-dart
pattern upon this moulding.

The term "development" is used to mean the un-
rolling of a curved surface, as if the surface of the
moulding were rolled out flat upon the paper. The
width of the development A m is equal to the length
of the arc, O, which may be found, either by meas-

uring the actual curve on the moulding with a strip
of paper, or by stepping off short portions of the arc
O with the spring compass, and taking their sum.

A m being made equal to the length of the arc, the
rectangle A H m n will represent a portion of the
developed surface of the moulding. We divide this
by vertical lines into sections A B, B C, etc., the width
of each being a little greater than the radius of profile
R to allow for width of darts. Then on alternate verticals B, D, F, and with the said radius, strike arcs
of circles tangent to the lower line m n.

From the centers of these circles draw arcs of smaller
circles to represent the edges of the deep grooves next
the eggs. Sketch in an egg, free-hand, as at F, making
it widest along the line of center O R, and tangent at
its lower end to the last arc drawn. Repeat the egg
on each of the dotted lines B, D, H, etc.; sketch in
the points of the tongues on C, E, G, etc., and also
indicate the drill holes.

Your egg-and-dart pattern should now be fitted to
the moulding, cutting the pattern along the lines A H
and m n, wrapping it against the ovolo, and pinning
so that an egg falls in the middle of the length of the
moulding. Repeat from the middle each way, to see
how the design "comes out." If it happens that the
eggs at the ends are cut by the miter, you must modify
your pattern so that the last egg will fall short of the
corner, as at W. The pattern can be "juggled" by
widening or narrowing each dart a trifle, and thus, by
repetition, shift the outer egg to the proper end position. When, by experiment, a satisfactory arrangement is found, the pattern is traced on the ovolo with

carbon paper, the "astragals," V, are sketched in to
center upon the eggs, and the pearls placed between.

Carving should begin by freeing the eggs with deep
gouge-cuts, and modeling them with bold strokes
downward into the grooves, the tool chosen to fit the
rounded surface of the egg, and pressed against it as
you make the slices. The center line of the eggs, B,
D, F, must always be left to preserve the profile of
the ovolo. Sink the darts and drill the holes above them,
but leave unfinished the ends of the moulding till it
is mitered and put in place where it is to remain. Then
a leaf pattern may be sketched and carved upon it as
shown at W, to cover the turn.

The ovolo, when made very wide, takes another
useful and bold pattern called the "gadroon," shown
in section in Fig. 48 at A, in front view at B and
development at C. The motive is a rounding projection shaped like a curved balloon or a carrot, repeated at intervals a little greater than the profile
radius R. The dotted lines p, q, r, show the spacing
of the gadroons, the semicircular heads being struck
with a radius half of R. These half-circles are pro-
longed with arcs of radius R, down to the lower line,
as shown at C. The wood between the gadroons is
now sliced out down to the dotted profile shown in A,
and the gadroons given an approximate modeling
while preserving, down the middle of each, the profile
surface of the original ovolo moulding.

Between the gadroons the leaf and V shapes are
sketched and carved, and the gadroons and other
curved surfaces are carefully finished, leaving, how-

ever, the two ends of the moulding untouched till put
in place, when the mitered corners may be carved with
a leaf, as shown at B. Generally a shield of some
agreeable shape occupies the center of the moulding,
and the gadroons radiate from it outward and upward
to right and left.

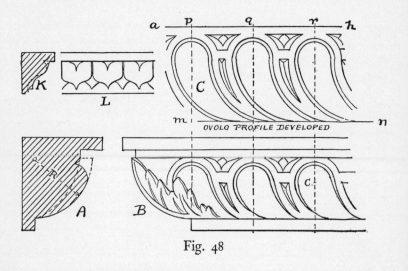

Fig. 48

The thumb moulding at D, Fig. 49, may be ornamented by a series of gadroons side by side, as at E,
with merely deep furrows between them. Another
treatment of this moulding is shown at F, copied from
our own dining table, where half-wheels are repeated
with triangular notches between. The three half-circles are merely grooved with the veining tool, and a
semicircular channel is slightly hollowed out and in
it a few crescent-shaped notches are cut with a small
gouge.

The cyma recta, G, may be enriched by carving a leaf pattern upon it known as an acanthus, shown in H, though bearing small resemblance to the leaf in nature. When this is to be done cut a small groove at the top, V, which represents the sinking of the ground back of the leaves, as shown in dotted lines in G. To determine the width of the repeat, draw a 45-

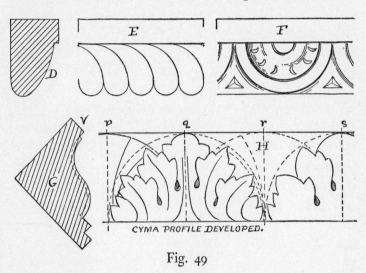

CYMA PROFILE DEVELOPED.

Fig. 49

degree miter line across the moulding, and take the length of it as that of half a leaf, or twice the length for a whole repeat. Develop the curve of the cyma, draw horizontal lines separated by this amount, and verticals, p, q, r, s, as in previous cases. Draw also half-circles between the horizontal lines, and sketch in the larger outlines of the front leaves, as at S, omitting the smaller serrations, sink the wood H between the leaves and sketch in the back leaves, giving them merely scalloped outlines, and suggestions of radiating veins, as at p. Sink the triangular spaces pq, qr to a deeper level. Now groove the veins of the front leaves with the veining tool, model them slightly so that lower lobes shall lap over upper ones, and finally cut all the serrations shown on the drawing. Leave the ends of the moulding uncarved till it is mitered and put into place, then a leaf may be carved on the corners with the miter as the midrib.

The small moulding shown in section at K and front view at L in Fig. 48 is useful for framing plain panels, and is exceedingly simple to carve. The profile K is called cyma reversa. Suggestions of leaves are sketched upon the curved surface. They are separated by narrow cuts, and their points are carved out; a tongue is left between the leaves, and a small triangle is cut in the upper middle of each.

The classical mouldings underwent modifications in course of time, and the designer will need to consider these variations, to adapt his mouldings to the style of work proposed. Architects who restore old Colonial houses are very particular to have the mouldings of the new woodwork conform, in profiles, with the old. These old mouldings were made with old-fashioned moulding planes, a collection of which is esteemed today a precious possession by the true craftsman. However, any contour can be reproduced by means of the "combination plane," provided the knife is shaped to give the profile desired. An expert machinist can file out any given profile on the knife of a plane.

Chapter XII

CARVED LETTERING

CHILDREN learning their letters are scarcely interested to know that their alphabet was taught by the Phœnicians to the Greeks and by the latter handed on to the Romans and thus distributed over the civilized world. And the student of wood-carving is likewise not interested in knowing that the square and erect type of Roman letters carved upon stone with the chisel gave us our capitals, while the "running hand" used in manuscript and written with the pen gave the small letters, called by the printer "lower-case" letters. But we see that the tool and the material decide the form of the letters, and the wood-carver is likewise influenced by his chisels and his wood in the choice of his style of inscription.

Mr. Lewis F. Day, in his book *Alphabets Old and New*, points out that lettering must first of all be legible, and, secondly, beautiful, but that the former quality should never be infringed upon by the latter.

The carver resorts to lettering more for a decorative purpose than to convey a message, and for this reason he is often tempted to obscure his text with excessive and tawdry embellishments. Clear and dignified letters, well spaced in words that are properly balanced in the phrases, produce beautiful and satisfying decorations.

For convenience we may classify lettering in four groups: the erect Roman, the inclined italic, the Gothic black-letter, and the decorative.

Letters may be either carved in relief or incised. In Fig. 50 Roman and Gothic letters I, O and S are taken

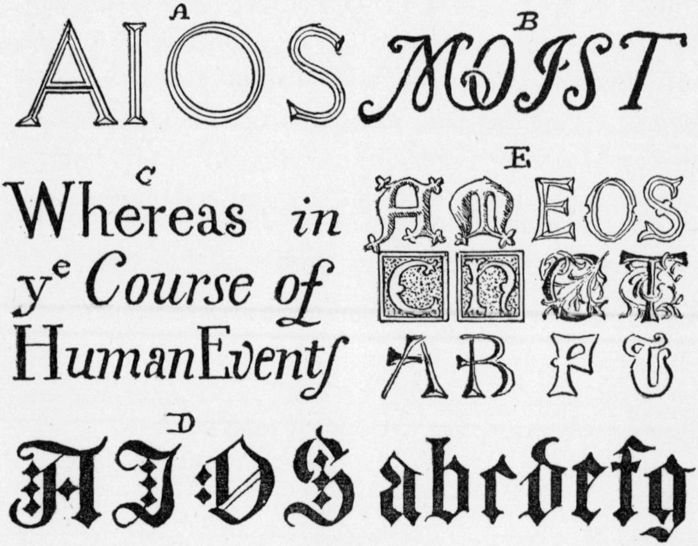

Fig. 50

as samples, as they contain most of the elements of the alphabet. If the inscription is to stand in relief, each letter is outlined with chisel cuts for straight parts, and gouge cuts fitting the curves. Then the ground is sunk to the proper depth, and the sides of all the letters are sloped off from the center lines downward and outward at an angle of 45 degrees. Since the grain of the wood naturally runs the length of the inscription, the vertical lines of the letters cross the grain at right angles and are likely to crumble away under the tool. Great care must be taken, therefore, in cutting the slopes, by making slices very thin.

Incising the same letters is a simpler matter, since the ground need not be cut away, and the letters cannot split off. Along the center line make a stop-cut the depth you can judge to be necessary and slice into this cut from each side, making the slopes approximate 45 degrees. The ends of the letters must be treated as one treats chip carving, by making stop-cuts in each little angle, and slicing out chips with the point of the carvers knife.

Another treatment for carving letters is a combination of the two foregoing methods called "cushioning," and consists in sinking the wood with a downward curve all around the edges of the letters, but leaving the spaces between the original surface while the center body of each letter is either grooved or hollowed.

Italic letters, B, are practically the same as the Roman, but are given an inclination of approximately 15 degrees. Lower-case letters may also be used in this type, and the capitals are ornamented with curves and flourishes. As the italics are derived from pen-work, the *downstrokes* are wider than the *upstrokes*, or the horizontal lines. Lettering peculiar to our Colonial period, to be found in old newspapers, upon old signboards and furniture, is a curious combination of both Roman and Italic, producing a singularly quaint and antique effect, as at C.

In a more pronounced degree we find this effect
in the Gothic, black-letter, or Old English lettering
which is distinctly the outcome of penwork, D. I
should recommend that the letters be always incised.
Do not attempt to cut them with the veining tool, for
in so doing at least half the cutting must be against
the grain. In the middle of each stroke make a stop-
cut, either straight or curved, and slice down into it
on a 45-degree slant. Chip-carve the tops and bottoms
where possible, then put in fine lines with the veining
tool.

Often an inscription is made up of a few elaborate
capitals followed by long lines of small letters, all the
latter of equal height. You can make rapid work here
by using a thin chisel and a mallet to make the vertical
stop-cuts down the center line of letters, then slice all
the right-hand slopes in succession, turn the work
about and slice all the remaining slopes. Make as many
slices as possible without changing tools; in this manner the work will progress with amazing speed, requiring only a few special curves and fine lines to finish.

Lettering cannot be sketched in free-hand with
success. It must be worked out on paper with considerable study and many changes. We are given a
certain length to fill with a certain text, composed of
letters and spaces. Most letters occupy equal spaces,
but i, j, l and t take only about half, and m and w
call for 1½ times the standard space.

Add up the letters, giving to each its unit or fraction
thereof, add spaces for the separations of the words,
and with this number divide up the whole length of

the inscription, marking off the divisions on a base line, and slightly sketching in every letter in its place.

The height of the letters is established by drawing a few different letters with great care and running a line along the tops of them, then fitting a few more letters to this height, to make sure it is good for all.

The entire inscription should now be drawn, and the effect studied as a whole. Here taste and judgment must be exercised, and improvements made, before tracing on the wood, for the effect desired is an artistic one, not to be obtained with square and rule.

The letters so far described have a certain geo-metrical basis, but in addition there is a vast family of alphabets which we might call the gypsies of the race. They wander picturesquely and appear in unexpected places, giving color and interest to their surroundings.

Artists of all times have exercised their playful fancies in embroidering the alphabet with their quaint conceits, and the resulting patterns are made available in many books, but few of these patterns are appli-cable to wood-carving. Some of the characteristic letters, borrowed from Mr. Day's book, are shown in E, Fig. 50, which will convey this decorative spirit. An inscription I planned to carve upon a wedding chest is shown in Fig. 51. It runs as a continuous band all around front and sides, just below the lid. The ground is sunk ¼ of an inch, and the letters, Gothic in character are formed by a continuous ribbon twisted and contorted so as to form a verse, familiar to most readers of poetry.

Though as a rule I am not in favor of the painting of

wood-carving, I have sometimes followed the example of illuminators of manuscripts and enlivened carved initial letters with bright colors and touches of gold

Fig. 51

leaf. In a dining room or a playhouse, appropriate mottoes so embellished add greatly to the atmosphere of festivity which should there prevail.

CHAPTER XIII

VARIOUS SUGGESTIONS

IT IS well to reserve a panel of wood as a kind of sampler, for experiments with tools and cuts, a kind of proving ground. We are apt to try out new cuts and odd motives upon stray blocks of wood which are often thrown away or lost. You should keep these experiments as records and reminders. A panel sampler, like the artist's sketchbook, becomes increasingly interesting.

Where we practice the hobby of wood-carving for our own enjoyment we are emancipated from restrictions imposed upon those who follow it as a business. We are free to draw our inspiration and obtain valuable suggestions from the work of the old master carvers. But we are also free to make use of modern appliances to help us in expressing our ideas. The band saw and turning-lathe are valuable and legitimate aids in making our work ready for the artistic treatment of our tools.

Sometimes the wood of a panel is very thin and needs strengthening to endure the heavy strokes of the mallet and carving tool. One writer suggests gluing the panel temporarily upon a more solid board for carving, *then splitting it off* with a broad, thin knife— a very dangerous process, likely to end in disaster.

Let me recommend that you choose a piece of thick brown wrapping paper and glue this between panel and board. When your carving is finished, you can split off your panel safely, for the brown paper, if of the proper quality, will split, one layer coming off on the panel, the other clinging to the board.

In case you want to make half-columns, or split moulds to use for iron casting, or quarter-rounds for carving as rope mouldings, this same method may be employed. We cannot turn on the lathe a half-round or a quarter-round, but we can prepare our wood in two sections or four, with thick paper glued between, and center the block on the line of joining. If there is danger that the parts may separate while in the lathe, this may be obviated by driving thin metal rings or "wiggle nails" into the ends of the wood.

Sometimes the mouldings around a panel are not mitered at the corners, but make the turn in a quarter-circle, with either an outward or an inward curve. We find the latter type in old furniture from Normandy or Brittany. In either case, the curved moulding may be turned as a ring on the face-plate of the lathe, using a carefully drawn template to give the desired profile, then sawing this into quadrants to fit the mouldings at the corners.

Let me remind you to make as many cuts as possible with one tool, and no change in position of the wood. And another useful hint: you naturally want all your stop-cuts to be made the same depth, so make a cut counting the strokes of your mallet, and see if you have gone the proper depth. If not, increase the number of strokes till you get the depth desired. After that, you can make all your stop-cuts with the same number of mallet strokes, with fair assurance that all are the same in depth.

Some time you will want to make an accurate copy of carving which you cannot take home for a model, as I had to do from a choir stall in a church. You can cover the carving with tissue paper to protect it, then press a thick layer of plasticine into all the crevices, and thus get a mould, into which you can pour plaster of Paris and get a fair cast to work from as a model. A few wrinkles and folds of the tissue paper will appear in the cast, but these may, of course, be omitted in carving the wood.

Breakage. Sometimes a faulty cut is made or a break occurs and the pupil believes his whole work ruined, and is consequently in despair. But there is no occasion for such discouragement, as there is the gluepot always at hand. I keep a little tin box ready to receive and preserve pieces broken off, which I can glue in place again after the carving is finished. Sometimes I hold the broken piece in place, drill a hole through it into the solid wood, and fix it with glue and a small dowel pin.

Where a portion of the design has been cut away inadvertently, a flat, smooth layer may be carved out, down to the background and a neat inlay be glued in, clamped and carved when thoroughly dry and firm. In performing this operation, the inlay must match the other wood as nearly as possible, and its grain lie in the same direction. If a crack or fissure occurs, you can glue a wedge into it and later carve it in a way to make the defect entirely disappear. We have no reason to suppose that the old master carvers were free from accidents in their manipulation of tools. Their works, now in the museums, exhibit many a break and scar, and it is quite possible that some of these are due to casualties in the carving, for it is evident that old repairs are likely to show themselves in course of time. Glue, subject to moisture, is sure to give way. For this reason it is preferable, in making our own repairs, to refrain from using a ready-made, liquid glue, and resort to hot glue, freshly dissolved, but never allowed to boil. There is a product now available known as "casein glue," a wonderful substance said to be made from cheese. It has the remarkable power of uniting two pieces of wood so firmly that they will break in some other place rather than separate, and is indifferent to moisture. I have two blocks, their grains united with casein glue end to end so firmly that I am not able to separate them even with a hammer.

In designing furniture, you will want the system of construction to correspond, in date, with that of the carving. The different phases of construction can be traced in the evolution of the chest. Beginning with a crude affair, hollowed out of the trunk of a tree, like an Indian "dugout" (from which, it is said, we derive the name "trunk" for our Saratoga or wardrobe trunk), the next form was a chest made of planks spiked or pegged together, their corners sometimes reinforced with iron work of more or less elaborate design.

Dovetailing was next employed to hold the corners together, and planks were united, edge to edge, by dovetail wedges.

Mortise and tenon joints were later used to frame together the parts of furniture, but pins were used to make them secure, without employing glue. This kind of joining should be imitated if your chest or "joint stool" belongs to that epoch.

As everybody knows, the object we want is always at the bottom of the chest. Hence, cabinetmakers soon introduced a drawer at the bottom of the chest, then a second, and a third; thus the "chest of drawers" came into existence.

In the construction of antique furniture screws were never used, and to use machine-made screws in a copy of an antique would appear a glaring anachronism.

To hold hinges and locks in place, rough, hand-wrought nails were employed, their points clinched on the inside. Hinges were often crude affairs, made by village blacksmiths, or their function was badly performed by staples. Nevertheless, in the fourteenth century we find hinges and ironwork in beautiful designs upon the furniture made by the hands of skilled craftsmen.

If you are working out a Gothic design, and wish your ironwork to carry out the period, you may like to use a method I saw practiced by an amateur carver, namely, the etching out of an intricate pattern. This is done by coating the iron plate with wax, back and front, scratching away the outline of the pattern down to the metal, then biting through it with acid and finishing up the edges with fine files.

There are many uses for our carving tools besides the embellishment of furniture and woodwork.

Cement, especially the White Atlas cement, is a beautiful, plastic material, often used in a crude and harsh manner, but capable of reproducing graceful forms and repeating them many times. In my garden are two seats in this material whose design I copied from the gardens of Versailles, carving the form, or mould, in pine wood so as to reproduce the classic original.

The severe, rectangular forms of flower boxes may be softened with a well-chosen ornament incised into the interior walls of the wooden form.

Cast iron is also a plastic and docile medium, susceptible of artistic and ingenious application, though few craftsmen think of employing it. Nearly every cast-iron object is made from a wooden pattern, often an elaborate piece of wood-carving. The old-time parlor and kitchen stoves, reeking with excessive ornamentations, were all cast from patterns carved in wood with skill, if not with art. In the huge fireplaces of European castles and manor houses are beautiful firebacks in cast iron, exhibiting heraldic arms and other devices, all of which were cast from their counterparts in carved wood. I made a large collection of photographs of handsome firebacks in France and England, and returning home, sought others of American fabrication but found only one in the Metropolitan

Museum in New York. For some unknown reason the firebacks were rarely made in this country, where they are quite as necessary to protect the bricks at the back of the fireplace. Here is an opportunity for the wood-carver to exercise his skill, in producing firebacks for his home. A bellows handsomely carved is a useful as well as ornamental implement for the fireside, but we may be hampered in making one for the want of an appropriate nozzle. Such was my case, and I was led to make a split pattern, by the brown-paper method; the tip I carved to represent a quaint head, like a gargoyle, the eyes protruding, the mouth open and the cheeks distended, as if vigorously blowing. The nozzle came back from our local foundry, its details perfectly reproduced in cast iron.

Embossed leather, made originally at Cordova in Spain, is a most luxurious and costly covering for furniture and walls. Here and there in castles and museums I have come upon this superb material and, while admiring the sumptuous coloring and gilding, I wondered how the embossing of the design was accomplished. The mystery was solved, however, when on a visit to the Victoria and Albert Museum, London, I discovered large blocks of wood beautifully carved with a sunken design intended for embossing the Cordova leather. On returning home, I cut a small block and, covering it with a piece of moistened leather, ran both through an etching press, and by the experiment proved that this simple process produced the embossed effect.

One of my pupils has discovered a use for wood-carving quite original with him. He has made jewelry of hard old mahogany, consisting of delicately carved beads for necklaces and exquisite pendent flowers for earrings. All were begun in the turning-lathe, the beads, carefully graduated as to size, were carved with intricate and delicate patterns, and strung with gold beads separating the wooden ones. The earrings, copied from the flower of the fuchsia, were given a calyx of gold, and a golden loop for the ear.

The wood-carver may use his tools to mark events in the family life, by making a "hope chest," like our frontispiece, a cradle or a high chair. Innumerable toys suggest themselves, as well as heads for puppet shows. I have seen an amusing set of chessmen, carved in characters from *Alice in Wonderland*. Wooden kitchen utensils may be embellished. There are rolling-pins carved with figures to be imprinted upon cakes and pastry, the designs and workmanship being of so high an order that these humble utensils are preserved in the Cluny Museum, Paris.

Wood-carving, which has become a mere industry in Switzerland, but a flourishing one, is practiced as a minor art in Germany, where Anton Lang, at Oberammergau, has won fame for his exquisite productions. In Venice the art is perpetuated by Signor Cadorin.

Perhaps we do not realize that the Indian totem poles are actually antique specimens of wood-carving, nor that there was a carver in every group of builders who migrated from town to town, erecting the fine, early American homes. In my boyhood nearly every tobacco shop had its wooden Indian, an antique now hard to find, and every sailing ship boasted of a carved figurehead, often of highly artistic merit. Though the art has fallen into disuse for want of patronage, we have in our country carvers of high ability and thorough training. I have already mentioned the work of Kirchmayer, and recommend you to study the beautiful carvings at Yale University, ornamenting the buildings of the Harkness Quadrangle and the Sterling Library, produced by expert craftsmen under the direction of the following contractors, who deserve mention because of the highly artistic standard of their work: Eli Berman Co.; Charles B. Mayer; George W. Smith and Martin J. Koehler. Their work is far above the commercial work executed by the machine.

There are many amateurs at work, here and there, enjoying the pursuit of carving as a hobby. When in time they can get together in a guild, as the Amateur Printers and the Amateur Photographers have done, when they hold reunions and exhibitions of their work, the art of wood-carving will come into its own, its beauty and importance will become appreciated. Thus it was that photography became elevated from a low ebb of commercialism, when amateurs took it up and for pure joy and delight developed its artistic possibilities. Exhibitions made so deep an impression upon the public that professional photographers were forced to accept artistic ideals and reform their technique.

Therefore, do not try to compete with the commercial carver. Set your own high artistic standard, and attain it through your enthusiastic endeavor. Yet in your enthusiasm, remember Rule No. III, and don't cut yourself!

BOOKS FOUND USEFUL AS A REFERENCE FOR THE WOOD-CARVER

AUSSEUR, ETIENNE, *La Menuiserie d'Art*. Paris: R. Ducher.

BINSTEAD, HERBERT E., *Useful Details in Several Styles*. London: Alfred H. Botwright.

Child and Universe, by Bertha Stevens. New York: The John Day Co.

CORNELIUS, CHARLES O., *Early American Furniture*. New York: The Century Co.

DAY, LEWIS F., *Alphabets Old and New*. London: B. T. Batsford.

——, *Ornamental Design*. London: B. T. Batsford.

ELLWOOD, G. M., *English Furniture and Decoration 1680-1800*. Stuttgart: Julius Hoffman.

GASCHET, HIPPOLYTE, *Manuel de Sculpture sur Bois*. Paris: Ballière et Fils.

GIBSON, KATHARINE, *The Goldsmith of Florence*. New York: The Macmillan Co.

JEFFREY, HENRY R., M. A., *Wood Finishing*. Peoria, Ill.: Manual Arts Press.

LOGNON, HENRI, and HUARD, FRANCES WILSON, *French Provincial Furniture*. Philadelphia: Lippincott.

MACQUVID, PERCY, "The Age of Oak," *Old English Furniture*. London.

ROE, FRED, R. I., *A History of Oak Furniture*. London: The Connoisseur.

ROWE, ELEANOR, *Practical Wood Carving*. London: B. T. Batsford.

SCHMIDT, HERMANN, *Das Mobelwerk*. Berlin: Ernest Wasmuth.

SIMMONDS, THOS. C., *Wood Carving*. London: George Allen & Unwin.

SMALL, TUNSTALL, and WOODBRIDGE, CHRISTOPHER, *Mouldings of the Wren and Georgian Periods*. London: The Architectural Press. New York: William Hilburn, Inc.

SMITH, H. CLIFFORD, M.A., F.S.A., *Catalogue of English Furniture and Woodwork*, in the Victoria and Albert Museum. London: Authority of His Majesty's Sationery Office.

VIOLLET-LE-DUC, M., *Dictionnaire Raisonné de l'Architecture*. Paris: A. Morel.

INDEX

Acanthus, 64
Astragal, 117

Boat motive, 83

Cabochon, 96
Cartouche, 37, 96
Carving in the round, 70
Cast iron patterns, 132
Cement casting, 132
Chip carving, 29
Chisels, 13
Culot, 93
Cuts, direction of, 5
Cyma recta, 119
Cyma reversa, 120

Designs, 50
Designs, enlargement of, 53
Development, 115

Egg-and-dart, 115

Fielded panel, 98
Fire-backs, 133
Flemish scroll, 101
Franklin stove patterns, 108

Gadroon, 117
Garrya elliptica, 107
Gibbons, 66
Gluing, 130
Gothic carving, 79
Gothic patterns, 82
Gouges, 13
Grinding, 19

Hands, position of, 6

Iron work, 131

Kirchmayer, 75

Lang, Anton, 134
Leaf-and-stick, 114
Leather embossing, 133
Lettering, 121
Linen fold, 85

Machine carving, 67
Mallets, 22
Modeling, 32
Mouldings, 110

Oil stones, 21
Ovolo, 115

Parchment fold, 52, 85
Pearls, 9
Pierced carving, 39
Pinnacles, 77
Plaster casting, 129
Pointed arch, 80

Renaissance carving, 90
Repairs, 129
Ribbon, 26, 112
Rocaille, 98
Rosettes, 10, 111

Sand paper, 19, 49, 68
Scraper, 17
Slice, 4
Special tools, 14
Spiral column, 102
Squints, 39
Staining, 47
Stop cuts, 4
Strapwork, 27
Sun-flower pattern, 106

Technique, 62

139

Thumb moulding, 118
Tool handles, 17
Tools, 12
Totem poles, 134
Toys, 73
Tudor rose, 105
Tulip pattern, 23, 106

Undercutting, 65

Varnish, 48

Woods, 41

Yule-log Box, 56